HOMING INSTINCTS

HOMING INSTINCTS

Early Motherhood on a Midwestern Farm

SARAH MENKEDICK

VINTAGE BOOKS

A Division of Penguin Random House LLC

New York

FIRST VINTAGE BOOKS EDITION, APRIL 2018

Some of the material in this book originally appeared, in slightly
different form, in *The Paris Review* and *Vela*.

The Library of Congress has cataloged the Pantheon edition as follows:
Name: Menkedick, Sarah, author.
Title: Homing instincts : early motherhood on a Midwestern farm /
by Sarah Menkedick.
Description: First edition. New York : Pantheon Books, [2017]
Identifiers: LCCN 2016034573.
Subjects: LCSH: Menkedick, Sarah—Family. Motherhood. Families.
Country life—Ohio.
Classification: LCC HQ759.M464 2017. DDC 306.874/3—dc23.
LC record available at lccn.loc.gov/2016034573

Vintage Books Trade Paperback ISBN: 978-1-101-97284-7
eBook ISBN: 978-1-101-87142-3

Author photograph © Jorge Santiago
Book design by Maggie Hinders

www.vintagebooks.com

Printed in the United States of America
10 9 8 7 6 5 4 3 2 1

For Dad, whose grace, empathy, kindness, and
humility I struggle to emulate.
This book is yours as much as mine.

En memoria de Doña Rosa,
con su gran corazón abierto y amoroso, quien
nos enseñó lo que más importa en esta vida

CONTENTS

HOMING INSTINCTS

HOMING INSTINCTS

THERE ARE five types of navigation, five means to find your way home: topographic, celestial, magnetic, olfactory, and true.

Topographic is used by the lowest forms of life, your mollusks and your limpets. Celestial is the rarest, wielded by some species of birds, some species of seals, certain humans, and the dung beetle. Many creatures finagle a combination: magnetic for broad route finding to general points, then olfactory for specifics.

True navigation can only be engaged in familiar areas, where one can rely on landmarks: roads, rivers, mountains, buttes, fields, forests, the abandoned house, the one-room Airport Inn, Stauf's Coffee, the water tower, the corner grocery, the place where memory has imprinted like the fuchsia or mournful blue on stained glass.

popped up around 2:00 p.m. to see if Jorge wanted to go
fishing and was pretty much wholly forgotten from that
point on. We end up in a natural rhythm, coinciding in
the space between house and cabin, by the garden or
chicken coop; calling one another up when we've made
stew; or—in Dad's case—sauntering up in his distinct
Dad way looking for a buddy to help saw wood or talk
turkey hunting. "Whoo boy," he begins, and he and Jorge
sit on the front porch like a pair of old-timers, squinting
at the sky, muck boots splayed before them, missing only
the overalls.

I am conspicuously not drinking, conspicuously quiet.
The Milky Way is out, a gossamer river poured across
the black country sky. There are coyotes howling, and the
echoes of owls sounding down the valley, but all of this
is static as I hurry single-mindedly through the pastures
toward the cabin.

Jorge and I brush our teeth while we wait. A clock
blinks on the test screen. It appears and disappears: *Wait,
wait, wait.* My heart gallops in that small yellow bathroom, though I don't really think it possible. I spit, rinse,
and look back.

"Oh my God," I say. "Oh my God. Oh, my God." I mean
it literally. It is not my usual easy expression of incredu-
lity or sarcasm. I am actually, in that moment, marveling
at some sort of higher power. I am clutching my stomach.
I am bending over. I am thinking, *I am actually going to do
this we are actually going to do this.*

At first it seems akin to the feeling I got the day I was offered a job in Beijing. I was sitting in front of Oaxaca's Santo Domingo Church when the university called and said I had the position teaching composition, and I thought, *We're going to China.* It is like this and yet, I quickly understand, not like this at all. It is not exterior but interior: a feeling in my gut, slung taut from hip bone to hip bone, of transformation. It is not so much a sense of being in control as of being taken over by a much-greater, daunting, awesome force.

That night Jorge puts his hand on my stomach, and we whisper about money, about names, about what it might be like, about the potential due date. I barely sleep, and in the morning I watch the blue light of early fall rise over the pastures. My body and mind are filled and fused with this secret, this knowledge, and I can think of nothing else. I am in awe that after all this time of wondering, fantasizing, vacillating, of swirling like a leaf in a whirlpool around the questions of home and children and change, suddenly a decision has been made, a physical decision with a heartbeat that now thunders at the core of my life.

I spend the first two weeks like this, unable to write, unable to think, unable to do anything but feel that tingly marvel of news. It is like being in a luminous tunnel, bedazzlement and hypnotic hum, free of time and space. And then I fall out the other side of it, and the architecture of my life collapses.

• • •

I was already taking my first vodka shot in the stuffy dorms of Madison, Wisconsin, while my dad was crying at the wheel on the way back to Ohio. Ever since I'd been old enough to grasp the notion of living on my own, I'd dreamed of escaping the dreaded Buckeye State.

I had a loving family, a lovely childhood. But I wanted out. I imagined my independence like a train barreling somewhere, anywhere, where I could create myself. Where I would be made real, new, free. Where I could do a twenty-seven-second keg stand and stay out until 6:00 a.m., then play delirious racquetball all morning, then run across a frozen lake; or where I could hop in a car and drive to the farthest corner of Texas to chase javelinas in the night and hike the barren, eerie, purple mountains along the border.

I started small, with Madison. Then France. Then Mexico, then Patagonia, then Réunion Island and China and Japan, the lines of my journeys tentative, then picking up speed, arching across the planet, pulsing on obscure islands. If I had been tagged, I would've been far out of range.

I missed births and deaths and graduations and recitals. I saw the photos, got the calls, sent congrats and consolation from cramped Internet cafés in Ushuaia and makeshift bamboo rooms by the south Indian sea. Talk of "family," "the importance of family," seemed absurd to me, as if family were an arbitrary and confining circle drawn in the sand.

"Family," and particularly the man-woman-child version, was the most traditional of concepts, the essence of the status quo. It was the core institution at the heart of all the institutions to which we are expected to conform: for family we do our homework and go to college and get a reliable job and make car payments and marry a nice man and have a baby and stick with our job and keep making car payments and send the baby to college and repeat. When I heard it evoked, it rang with near-mythical responsibility, an überstructure we must obey, like the KGB or the IRS. I say this coming from a family that is unusually close and like-minded, one of inside jokes and dynamic conversations and genuine intimacy; it is not that I've felt trapped by my specific set of parents and siblings but rather by the concept and its demagogic invocation.

I loved my family, but I also loved the jostling of a bus across the altiplano, the distinct sense of myself in the world away from the limiting molds of familial roles, and the characters I formed friendships and relationships with over the course of continents and years. The challenges lay elsewhere, humped in an undulating line like dunes extending to a vanishing point. My job was to tackle them one after the other. Home was too easy.

What I failed to recognize, but increasingly discern like a new delicacy in the air just before summer, are all the complex interior workings of family, the way our homes are written on us and we on them, and the increasing need over time to study these inscriptions, heed them, test them, learn them like a sacred text. Eventually, after so many years of travel, I reached the point where my self—the one who wandered alone through the gray foreign streets of Bogotá, the one who ran in the blue dawn on the frayed white edge of an island, the one who flirted with an Argentine in a frigid Chilean cabin, the one with all of her clever noticing of striking detail— had become boring. She began to seem like the handful of go-to phrases I first mastered in Spanish—*tengo que, voy a*—phrases that at a certain point could no longer express three-quarters of what I wanted to say. Beyond them I could sense an entire language, with all of its intricate meanings and signifiers, that I couldn't yet speak. Beyond that self lay an interior, familial morphology of blood and muscle, memory and longing, a terrain mappable less by active thought than by absorption, in the same way that language cannot be directly translated but must be felt.

Salmon are born in freshwater rivers at high altitudes and spend their first months or years in the relative safety of their natal rivers, camouflaged by brown-black stripes that mimic the moving chaparral cover of the water. Fitting in and staying alive are paramount in these years: only 10 percent of the young fish will ever make it to sea.

Those that survive are called smolts, gaining brilliant silvery scales that are easily rubbed off. They move into brackish waters to begin acclimatizing themselves to the salty sea, where they'll finally earn the title of salmon. Then they'll spend up to five years in the open ocean, gradually reaching sexual maturity. When they're ready to spawn, the salmon turn around and travel hundreds of miles back to their natal rivers, to the very spots where they were conceived years ago. They form massive salmon runs upriver, leaping as high as twelve feet over rapids and waterfalls, some snapped up by fishermen and grizzlies before their destinations. Once they make it home, they reproduce and promptly die, their gaping, hook-jawed skeletons disintegrating in native waters, and the cycle repeats itself.

The salmon find their way back through all that choppy, anonymous ocean to the alpine niche of their creation via a process called magnetoreception, or magnetic navigation. The earth's equator can be imagined as a bar magnet, which sends magnetic waves southward; these waves then curve back northward and hit the earth at an incline. The waves that hit closest to the equator have almost no incline; those that hit closest to the poles have the steepest inclines. The salmon have imprinted the particular incline waves of home, the so-called magnetic footprint of their birthplaces, in much the same way that a certain species of Ohioan is engraved with the insistent pulsing of crickets or the smell of a musty basement or the feel of rushing downhill on a sled with a soaring heart. Imprinting has three characteristics: it has to occur during a particular critical period, usually early in the life of the animal; its effects last a long time; and these effects cannot be easily modified.

Singing "America the Beautiful" on our octogenarian neighbor Herman's doorstep in exchange for strawberry-flavored, diabetic hard candies, or the view out our kitchen window onto bare branches and that eggshell-thin winter sky, or the scraping of the skateboard as it picked up speed on our sloped driveway. The one-hundred-mile stretch between Columbus and Cincinnati: corn and sky, barn and highway. Dad's backpacking vacations, the film containers of salt and pepper, the rasp of cards being shuffled, caves and creeks and boots with red laces.

So this magnetic imprint, activated by the procreative urge to return home after so many years adrift in the great beyond, guides the salmon to the mouths of their rivers or the general vicinity, but what takes them all the way back, to the very spot, to the cradle where it all began and will end, is smell.

The air when I land at the Columbus airport, at night, and roll down the window as we wind around the parking-garage ramp: In summer, like water from the tap, wet bark, full bloom. In winter, sharp with ice and woodsmoke, a little dagger in the sinuses. The Bath & Body Works ginger perfume I doused myself with during high school as if it were some sort of protective coating against a deadly virus. Cut grass. Clover. The faint mud musk of the fall woods. Sprinklers; wet sidewalks; the bitter, pollen-heavy scent-shock of a dandelion. The thick, sour hops of my niece and nephew's hair.

The hen is not budging. Hell, no. We reach out to touch her and get a long peeved *squaaaaaaaawk* as she settles herself in deeper. Days like this: not eating, not drinking, yanking out her own feathers to insulate her young. "She's gone broody," my stepmom tells me and several friends of mine. We've come out together from Pittsburgh for a weekend visit to the farm, toting our printed pages of workshop essays.

Broodiness is the maternal instinct turned pathological: a neurotic self-flagellation not unlike that of today's supermoms. My parents put the hen in a dog kennel and dump a bucket of cold water over her. That's it: she is cured of broodiness. *What in the hell was I thinking?* we ventriloquize in her high clucking hen voice. *So much time with those ungrateful little brats?* She goes back to merrily plucking up grubs like nothing has happened.

My friends and I, meanwhile, at the time rooted in graduate school and sensing ourselves on the fulcrum between twenties and thirties, begin using the ominous declaration "She's gone broody" to announce those periods when we do not move from our desks, when all we want to do is go home and stew over book-babies. It is

to a nontemporary plan, don't know what this will feel like and what weight it will carry, whereas I know very well the emotional and practical shape of landing in utter unfamiliarity and working my way into understanding, loving and resenting, moving on and missing.

Throughout my years in Pittsburgh, I wonder if the attraction to rootedness is simply a passing fancy, not so different from my other standby fantasies of becoming a park ranger or diplomat or tour guide on remote South American rivers. Sometimes I think I can shake it off like a dog shedding water in a vigorous spray. I think I *should* shake it off, lest it entrap me. I know so little about this new type of unknown that I cannot begin to discern the outlines of the knowledge and change it might bring. I look as hard as I can, but no clear picture coheres, and I go back to my stack of musty library books, back to my thesis, back to afternoon walks with the dogs, through which flit familiar visions of future glory.

During the final stretch of graduate school, I write an email to a friend in which I say that my postgraduation plan involves one of two options: a baby or a year-long trip through Africa. In truth I have made zero steps toward either, but the hyperbolic declaration seems right for this moment of ambiguity. It represents the difference between a cycle and novelty I know so well, and one that beguiles, haunts, and repels.

"Only you," the friend writes back, "would face that choice."

And I feel a little shine of pride, a pleased flutter of the ego, before I remember that my friend, too, and pretty much every woman I know—mostly career travelers, sure, but also the less internationally inclined—is facing this choice. The specifics may vary, but on one side of the scale sits the freewheeling twentysomething intellectual and her creative and aesthetic pursuits, and on the other a chunky toddler proffering a dandelion. The hazard of the former is a growing sense of avoidance, of dodging challenges and questions bigger than any language or custom; the hazard of the latter might just be my entire life and self.

Even the spiny lobster—an invertebrate that, in the terms of a researcher dedicated to its study, is essentially a "big ocean insect"—has complex navigational systems for finding its way home. In 2003, biologists Kenneth Lohmann and Larry C. Boles of the University of North Carolina at Chapel Hill published the results of a study showing that spiny lobsters are capable of measuring minute changes in the earth's magnetic field in order to make their way back toward their dens. Boles caught more than one hundred spiny lobsters off the coasts of the Florida Keys, put them in opaque compartments suspended by ropes, and took them on roving, erratic, unpredictable journeys by boat and car back to laboratories between seven and twenty-three miles from the capture sites. "I was worried about attracting attention from the marine patrol looking for drunken boaters," Boles told *Science*.

Back at the lab, with the absurd, loving devotion of the scientist, Boles fashioned teensy caps out of dental amalgam and used these to blind their protruding lobster eyes. He then set them down in a tank on the floor and found that they invariably scraped their newly landlocked way toward their particular patches of sea. If they'd been taken at 250 degrees north, for example, they aimed at an average of 220 degrees north, no matter how much they'd been shaken and rocked and twisted during their journeys.

The fact that the lobsters could navigate homeward even after extreme disorientation implies, Boles told *National Geographic,* "that they somehow know where they are all the time, that something is built-in."

Boles and his partner then tested the lobsters' magnetic navigation by wrapping a magnetic coil around their tanks. Via the coil, they simulated the conditions of magnetic fields far from Florida. The lobsters whose simulated fields were north, walked south; those whose fields were south, walked north.

The captive lobsters, said Boles in a press release, "acted as if they were at the location that the magnetic field represented and ignored their actual physical location."

The lobsters' navigational systems, their desire to get back to the murky dens of their unique coral reefs, overrode the tumult of their journeys and the facts of the dank laboratory before them in favor of interior signals. They pivoted, scrabbled, and scratched their antediluvian claws on the floor, finessing their naked skeletons and probing antennae back to that one brackish patch, its magnetic symbols emanating from the core of the earth, saying, *Here, here.*

There is a particular feeling around family, like a miasma, background and elusive but ever present. It is the sense that, for as much as we talk—and there is plenty of that, shouted over the rush of small children, tossed back and forth on forest trails, parried over a platter of char-grilled meats—talk is superfluous. The specific nature of the encounter or the conversation is secondary to the fact of simply *being with family.* With similar cells coursing through our bodies, and having spent some ungodly number of hours together in carpeted old vans and duct-taped tents and small kitchens in the middle of winter, we have to do nothing more than sit and eat baked beans to achieve communion. Family gives us likeness and ease: the tame, antichallenge of literal familiarity.

But perhaps there comes a time when we are not searching for the same types of challenges, and our priorities shift. The challenges lie not out there, always a little farther, on the bright horizon of independence, but closer to home, deeper and murkier and less immediate. The larger questions that have stewed beneath the definable challenges of education and acculturation and career now become palpable and inescapable. Wherever we go and whatever we seek, we sense them beneath us.

• • •

In much the same way that a painting or poem seems straightforward until one learns more about painting and poetry ("Yeah, I've thought about writing," a lawyer friend told me once, offhand, as if it were a career path he could've taken straight to the Pulitzer if he'd merely indulged his whim), familial ease is simple to shrug off as given until we start paying attention. Then family becomes a dynamic studied and sought, an answer to a question we haven't quite figured out how to ask.

To stay home—*to home*—is to cultivate a different kind of attention. It is to notice more acutely, with an interior radar: the warm and unstudied composure of my sister as she enters her forties and grows into herself; the hint of old Cincinnati in how my dad says "warsh," just like my grandmother did; the photos of my stepmother Meg's mother, who died young, framed and set on the marbled wardrobe in Meg's bedroom; the ways we echo or surprise each other; the places we clash and the places we move easily together; the moment on the gravel driveway watching my nephew Mario take aim with a BB gun at a grizzly Jorge has drawn on a sheet of paper, all of us lined up in a row, sloping in parallel with the trees, arms draped across one another.

In my twenties it seemed everyone I knew had a gaggle of diverse friends, all of whom were rushing through identities and possibilities and dreams, but as we steady into our ways, become more predictable and singularly focused, many of these connections grow more threadbare, less relevant: they get stuck in the shallows of our deepening and narrowing. Or we simply move away.

There is not the same push for effervescent conversation or novelty or excitement as there is for someone to talk to for hours about the fear and hope of babies or the problem of writing point of view. We couple up, go to graduate school, launch careers: our interests and lives taper from a delta of options into a directed watercourse. We seek friends who will feel like family. Settled now into ourselves, rooting like a river into its banks, we search for what stays, for familiar cartographies.

Herpetologist Archie Carr, a key figure in Caribbean conservation projects and the establishment of Costa Rican national parks, was one of the first to recognize homing instincts in turtles. His book *The Windward Road* recounts a story he heard from several fishermen, which got him interested in turtle navigation. Green turtles had been captured in their feeding grounds, branded with the fishermen's initials, and put on a boat headed for Key West. The boat capsized in a storm, and months later, the fishermen discovered the branded turtles back in the same spot off the Nicaraguan coast. Dr. Carr stipulated that green turtles had an "extra sense," what we now recognize as a homing instinct, "that lets them make long, controlled journeys in trackless seas."

The homing instincts of the eponymous pigeon—

a crucial historical figure that has announced the results of Roman chariot races; relayed updates throughout Genghis Khan's empire; spied for the Germans and rescued French battalions in World War I; and today spots shipwrecks from U.S. helicopters and ferries blood samples across Europe—are still not well understood. The pigeons might use the sun or, when it's cloudy, rely on magnetic navigation; the small deposits of iron in their beaks might act as a compass; they might navigate using sound or smell.

Then again, they might just take the damn highway. A 2004 Oxford University study, the culmination of ten years of careful tracking of homing pigeons with tiny GPS devices, concluded that the birds aren't using the mystical powers of magnetoreception but are instead sailing right along the road.

"It is striking to see the pigeons fly straight down the A34 Oxford bypass, and then sharply curve off at the traffic lights before curving off again at the roundabout," Professor Tim Guilford told the *Daily Telegraph*. For as much as the scientists sought a complex hidden mechanism, an intricate mystery to be methodically unraveled, the pigeons' journeys were as simple and straightforward as the well-traveled highway, more common than unique, more ordinary than exceptional.

I know I've been in the United States too long when, during my last semester of graduate school, I have a wispy, romantic moment in the Target parking lot. I'm gazing at a hazy summer-green hill in the distance, and I daydream of mashing up Cheerios for a baby and sitting around in the warm fading light doing little other than being home.

That's when I open the car door for my husband and say, "We should move to Borneo."

This yen for the domestic has the swell of a biological urge, like thirst or the pressure to urinate, and thus seems potentially suppressible. But between the billows of fantasy, easily written off, lingers a more complicated longing. It is not related to one particular place but rather to the idea of a place that could be mine. Of a different kind of familiarity and fondness: not the traveler's ready-made nostalgia, in which each detail of daily routine is exceptional in its temporality, but a rhythmic seasonal understanding, an accumulation of memories like the analogous images that compose a Magic Eye picture and occasionally cohere into a lucid, surprising whole-ness. Lately, on these cornflower-blue midwestern evenings, a train shuddering under the pedestrian bridge, I've realized how much of the thrill I get from being in a certain place comes from projecting myself into the near future when I will not be there and will instead be looking back. I wonder what it would feel like to have no plans for an elsewhere or a new destination; to be bound and beholden to the rhythms of one place; to accept it as home, now, everyday.

I've had many pretend homes, pretend lives. Pretend not in the sense that they weren't real but rather that they

9:00 a.m. in an empty restaurant while reading Haruki Murakami.

Seeing, I might have answered her. Using myself like a Monopoly piece, moving around the world to acquire experience and knowledge. Discovering, occasionally, the capacity for a self-annihilating humility that would serve me later. Marveling at the sheer possibilities of one life while sitting on the balcony of the half-built villa two friends and I rented at cut-rate prices and carved up with bamboo dividers, watching the ocean fade into blue and the wet heat of the day creep sticky and thick over the island. Stepping out of my tent in Cilaos to discover the moon hanging like a bell above the darkened ranges, the haunted blue of the dawn, the world suspended. Finding that vanilla is brown and spindly and tough. Melting fresh dates into bars, ordering *bière à la pêche,* waving a silent hello to the old Creole men and women submerged in the early-morning surf.

Sometimes, I blended with the world, I felt myself nearly disappear, I crossed the line from observing and narrating to fading into the moment. Nearly always this happened on mountains. In the Peruvian Andes near the summit of a peak I'd somehow convinced a pudgy British software engineer to tackle with me, I settled in high grasses and watched fog wash over the slope. Huddled amid the watery sound of wind moving through grass, I felt myself a vessel, a presence no more present than rock or air. In Patagonia I sang as loud as I could at the top of a peak in Parque Nacional Los Alerces, the Patagonian wind whisking away my cheesy, tuneless lyrics as soon as they emerged, but instead of an act of assertion it felt like one of erasure, like being so alone and so high up and so far I lost all the markers of self completely.

And yet also, all this time, I yearned for something more, which I found in writing. I wrote horrible blog posts, horrible essays, horrible metaphors, the kind of pieces I cannot even visit now without wanting to evaporate in self-loathing. I was "finding my voice," as they say, but more than that I was feeling through all the noticing, all the novelty of experience, toward the more nebulous, universal, and personal. Writing drove through the trophy hunt of experience toward bigger questions and themes, and eventually, one morning in Beijing, I announced to Jorge that I wanted to stop seeking the teaching jobs that allowed me to leap from country to country and instead return to Mexico to write. In a trajectory I could not intimate at the time, travel led me to writing, and writing led me home.

Sitting in the mornings on the cabin porch, glassy eyed before the scramble of words on the page, I envy writers like Joan Didion, who belong so clearly to and are so clearly of a place, who rise like apparitions from it and might later earn a roadside plaque. I don't yet know how to do or write that kind of relationship. I struggle to see home—the unseen blue screen behind all the travel narratives that have made me a writer—as I've seen abroad. Where Mexico offers up its bloody crucifixion scenes and its bawdy teenage clowns in a screaming panorama, Ohio is hard to see at all. I pile my desk with guides to midwestern birds and trees and grasses to help bring the life on these forty acres into relief. My new *Lonely Planet* is a well-thumbed copy of native wildflowers, dog-eared not at Inner Mongolian hostels but at violet wood sorrel, found on open prairie and rocky creek banks. I try to learn Ohio in the same way I learned to order Chinese noodles, not yet grasping that I need a new paradigm, a new way of noticing and being.

Didion's relationship with California was wrought, at times as sour and acrid as the burning Santa Ana winds, at others driven by bittersweet and tender longing for those winds. I wonder if part of this complexity stems from the shame of the ambitious young woman at returning to the nest, although I suppose that shame is blunted when the nest is New York or Los Angeles.

Ohio, meanwhile, is a place the ambitious and creative are meant to escape and then look wryly back on from one of the coasts. But regardless of the cultural desirability of one nest or another, it is still the nest, and the singular aim of savvy young women in particular is to flee it. So when the homing instincts kick in, they are bound to come with undertones of capitulation and failure: *I didn't make it far enough, didn't push or try hard enough.*

I couldn't cut it, make myself anew. For as much as we extol women's hard-won right to choose, we still tend to notice the women who have chosen to live like men: untethered to the domestic, to home, beholden instead to a sense of exploration, discovery, and achievement.

In Beijing, Jorge and I sometimes left the house at 10:00 a.m. and returned at 10:00 p.m., having spent the entire day walking the streets, stopping for meat kebabs and sesame rolls and beer, watching the city unfold around us. In South America I spent weeks on buses, rolling into one station only to stumble toward the counter for another ticket, buy a few empanadas of enigmatic filling, and roll out southward. Once, on a bus in Colombia, after an unknown stretch dipping and weaving through green mountains, we stopped at a small roadside cafeteria. It was pouring rain. The driver escorted me to and from the restaurant with his umbrella. I remember only that: the bus, the mountains, the rain, the gesture. These years were composed of elements, details, the press of the world onto my skin, my pressing back. Perhaps this experience was the currency I needed to buy the confidence to write, and once I learned to write and to see anew, experience was no longer everything.

As I near graduation in Pittsburgh, I wonder if writing has really come to be enough: if I don't need Mexican taxis or unmarked Chinese trails as much anymore because the act of putting words on a page before a discerning editor is sufficiently hair-raising and offers my life a deeper quality of noticing than scrambling perpetually up new heights of adventure. When I first began writing, I thought that the experience fed the page, that I would always need to go farther and do more to fill that blank space. Instead, the more I write, the less I need the glaring eccentricities of abroad, the amulets and trains and floodlit beaches.

I am reluctant, however, to let them go. I don't want to go broody; I still want my curiosity, want to roam. I understand how transforming travel and unfamiliarity can be, how they can challenge a dangerous and stultifying complacency. I don't want to sink into the antiquated responsibilities that have long prevented women from being seen or heard. But I am newly compelled by these responsibilities. I find in them a dignity and meaningfulness I did not ten, five, two years ago. I find in them, even, the big questions about how I want to see and live. I recognize that interior mechanism pointing back home: its stubborn innateness, the map that defies all maps. I turn back with more regularity, more gratefulness, for longer and longer stretches, letting myself go.

Dung beetles are highly competitive; when one encounters a pile of dung, it has to roll up a little ball and move that ball away as fast as possible or other dung beetles will come along and swipe it. It's far easier to swipe someone else's ball than to roll your own, and courtesy has not been evolutionarily rewarded among dung beetles.

The fastest route away from dung-robbers-in-waiting is a straight line, which the beetles follow while pushing their balls facing backward, eyes always on the receding mound of loot. "If [you] roll back into the dung pile, it's curtains," biologist Eric Warrant warns in *National Geographic*. Scientists, wondering how the beetles could stay such a direct course without seeing it, designed an experiment to test beetle navigation. The scientists built tiny cardboard and plastic hats for the dung beetles, like miniature visors of the type seen on befuddled dads at amusement parks. The beetles with the cardboard hats took far longer to navigate at night than those with the transparent ones, and even under a slightly cloudy or moonless sky the transparent-visored beetles rolled faster. The beetles, the scientists concluded, navigated using the Milky Way.

The scientists also discovered that whenever the beetles hit snags on their routes, they stood atop their balls of poo and "danced" to the stars, turning round and round until they oriented themselves by galactic light.

Unlike other animals, which might simply give up after a certain number of meddlesome scientific intrusions, the dung beetles will keep on trekking even when scientists put them on circular tracks or drop them off ledges.

"They are so tenacious in what they are trying to do. They cannot be distracted, they don't get frightened, they don't change their minds, they don't get stage fright. They are so, so, so determined," zoologist Marcus Byrne told the *New Yorker*. For what is at stake is nothing more or less than home: the secure ball will attract a mate, who will lay an egg inside it. When the egg hatches, it eats its way out, emerging from its snug dung home to face the fervent competition of the wider world, and the cycle repeats itself.

When I was young I used to travel each weekend from Columbus, where I lived with my dad and stepmom, to Cincinnati to visit my mom. The Ohio landscape was a flat canvas outside, sometimes minimalist in Rothko squares of hay and navy, sometimes dramatic Constable-inspired landscapes of clouds: massive ships with violet underbellies sailing against the gunmetal of thunder-storms. These panoramas were interrupted here and there by outlet malls and DQs and reminders that HELL IS REAL. I remember once being in the backseat of the Toyota Tercel in the middle of a summer storm. I don't remember which way we were going, north or south, toward or away from the Washington Court House exit off I-71, where Dad handed me over to Mom and vice versa, but I remember feeling safe. Not the kind of safe that is pitted against danger, but the kind of safe that is cozy and secure, existentially safe as if nothing else—school or dinner or leaving one parent behind for the other—mattered, because I was in this moving car with someone who loved me and whom I loved and there was a vibrant storm outside.

I feel the same kind of safe again in the Pittsburgh summer in my and Jorge's boiling apartment, when I go upstairs after I've spent the morning writing and open the door to the cool bubble of the bedroom, where the ancient air conditioner throbs with its expulsion of chill, and where Jorge and the dogs lie in a cold mess on the rumpled sheets. It is a sensation that comes only with being closed in, homed in, the boundaries between myself and the world very clearly defined, narrow, containing only me and my family.

I have spent so much of the last decade searching for this sensation's polar opposite: the sense of vastness, wideness, the enormity and potential for infinite variation of the world. Backpacking alone in Patagonia to feel not safe but free, discovering my small, fleeting insignificance in a huge world of gray stone and pink sky and blue ice. Throwing myself at mountains and rugged shorelines, at the unknowable, in order to sense the tininess of my own existence, in order to blur and render insignificant the intricate roots and details that bind me to the everyday and to home: to feel, in other words, the big picture.

In the last semester of graduate school, I open the fridge and root around for leftover brownies. I stand by the window drinking a glass of cold water and smelling the sour tang of mulberries finally ripened, I walk in the afternoon with the dogs to the big grassy hill at a nearby university, I sit and watch the same minor duckling dramas in the same small koi pond, I lie in bed all afternoon rereading *Lolita* and enjoying the whiff of barbecue from a backyard grill nearby, I stand on the pedestrian bridge and watch the trains hurtle by beneath me.

Soon, I will gather up our boxes of books and Ikea dishes and dog toys and move with Jorge into the cabin, built in 1828, smelling of the sturdy wood planks that compose its walls and floors. I will set my desk before the front window and begin to write in the perpetual semidarkness, amid a palimpsest of quaint domestic objects belonging to other times and people: baskets, hand-painted serving platters, quilts, crocks. Everywhere around me dangle the artifacts of women's work—the churning and the storing and the serving and the healing. I stand on the front porch, barefoot and comically aware of my barefootedness, surveying the land from this small refuge, aware only in the faintest of stirrings that these forty acres will become home in a way no place has ever been.

Adulthood, it seems to me, is about narrowing. The salmon roams the vast Pacific and then, to the thrum of its own programmed brain, begins its journey in a shrinking triangle closer and closer to the river mouth, then up the river, then over the falls, then into the forest to that one tapering stretch that is now its focus, center, and range.

JOURNEY INTO THE ORDINARY

I F IT HITS, it'll hit like a ton of bricks," the ob-gyn advises at my first, five-week appointment. She is talking about nausea and the bundle of unpleasant symptoms that make the first trimester a notorious trial period, but she might as well be speaking of a paradigm shift in my life.

I assume, both when Jorge and I decide to give it a go in September and when we find out I'm pregnant in October, that I'll continue with my life more or less unaltered for the next nine months, until the baby arrives and brings all the changes we've heard so much about: the sleepless nights, the overwhelming love, the schedules and work and relationships turned inside out and upside down. Even in those initial weeks, when we return again and again to the bathroom to raise the stick to the light and stare at its unequivocal YES, when I cannot concentrate on writing a hundred words, cannot read or think straight, I somehow maintain this belief. I hold to a pleasant bucolic vision of steadiness, as if I'll just transition from riding through the Mexican jungle in the back of a pickup to twenty-four-seven childcare in a rustic Ohio cabin like crossing the border from one country to another. It isn't until I open the fridge one day and want to hurl at the sight of eggs that I begin to understand the change isn't something neatly prolonged and prepared for but immediate, all-consuming, and violent. It is the kind that wrenches us completely from the stories we have long told about ourselves, and rewrites us.

Earlier that summer, sitting on a boulder in the middle of a creek in the White Mountains, I'd come to the realization that both of my parents changed dramatically at age thirty-one. My little brother, Jackson, a jazz musician with whom I'd long shared grand artistic aspirations and dubious financial prospects, had announced on a whim in June that he was driving across the country, stopping for weeks at a stretch to backpack the national parks, and—as he put it in his earnest and guileless Jack way—"figure some shit out." He was armed with Dad's moldering backpacking gear, a copy of the *Tao Te Ching*, and an industrial quantity of Great Value peanut butter. I immediately latched on to the plan, begging him to let me come for two weeks, which is how I wound up deep in the White Mountains in August, talking Tao and art and life with Jack, eating a lot of ninety-nine-cent pasta singles. In this exhausted satisfaction of hikes and books, I read the insight about my parents as an indication that I should become more attuned to the natural world: not just a weekend worshipper of mountains and woods, but someone who knew the names of the mushrooms and the calls of the birds. This was the kind of change I was familiar with: apply oneself to a new learning curve, develop a new skill set, and voilà: a measurable self-improvement. I missed the arduous transformation my parents had undergone and saw instead the type derived from New Year's resolutions: me plus French, or me plus extensive knowledge of tree species, or me plus marathon training.

In retrospect, this insight about my mom and dad, which lifted unbidden out of that creek of piebald boulders, is much more prescient. When they were thirty-one, my parents divorced. My dad took me and moved to inner-city Cincinnati. He sought refuge in the natural world, rebuilding himself with backpacking trips around Ohio and Kentucky, where he taught me about hemlock tea, sassafras, maple, and oak. He led the Cincinnati chapter of the Sierra Club's Inner City Outings, guiding rowdy groups of kids on expeditions into the midwestern woods. He meditated, read, raised me, and worked his way through devastating loneliness in our dark basement apartment on Ravine Street. By the time he met Meg, my future stepmom, he was no longer the working-class Ohio dad who'd given up a full scholarship to Northwestern to marry my mom, have a baby, and work nights at a Cincinnati grocery store. He was no longer poker-playing, Bud-drinking, handlebar-mustache-and-running-shorts Dad. He and Meg adopted a Buddhism-influenced Eastern religion that inspired them to move to the countryside in Indiana, become vegetarian, hand stencil old furniture with psychedelic suns, and—briefly—take up O'Douls. They had my little brother and built a life of medita-tion, weekend hikes, hippie casseroles, beat-up vans, and Dwight Yoakam.

Eventually, they distanced themselves from the reli-gion, but the change stuck. The dad I know and remem-ber is this dad, who finds solace and nourishment in the woods; who listens to tapes of turkey calls and answers them with his own turkey call, which hangs from a cord around his neck; who is deeply influenced by Buddhist thought. My sister, ten years older than me, has known two dads. They share certain characteristics—unflagging optimism; a profound and gentle intelligence; the ten-dency to make enormous piles of "slop," a conglomera-tion of lima beans heaped on corn heaped on rice that seems suited to a trough—but they are in many ways dif-ferent people.

My mom, meanwhile, left behind Pleasant Ridge and her roots as part of a stern, conventional, working-class German family to explore Europe and become a willowy, bohemian beauty I idolized throughout my childhood. She went to the symphony, wore vintage dresses with scalloped collars and tiny waists, and took me to downtown coffee shops thick with smoke and chatter. She lived in an old brick house on the cusp of Cincinnati's downtown and let me write on its peach walls. In her kitchen, with its view of an old sycamore and Cincinnati's steep hills, I discovered Gouda cheese and grainy Dijon mustard with seeds. She'd yanked herself out of the trajectory of young, taciturn motherhood and work for work's sake but still sought a clear sense of purpose. Sometimes amid the elegance of her house, or in the backyard, looking at the distant railroad tracks tinged blue in winter, I sensed her loneliness.

Thirty-one was the year that rewrote both their lives.

My thirty-first year begins with the physical onslaught of pregnancy. Susan Sontag famously wrote, "Illness is the night side of life, a more onerous citizenship. Everyone who is born holds dual citizenship, in the kingdom of the well and in the kingdom of the sick. Although we all prefer to use the good passport, sooner or later each of us is obliged, at least for a spell, to identify ourselves as citizens of that other place." Pregnancy is not illness, but the way it plunges women into the realm of the physical, placing the body at the forefront of experience, mimics illness's disorienting and drastic perspective shift. Like many young people, I had taken my body for granted, dwelling almost wholly in my mind and its warren of obsessions, hopes, and worries. I focused on my body during a long run or while pulling a skirt over my hips, but this awareness was considered and temporary. Pregnancy, however, shoves my body and its complex machinations onto center stage, making it impossible to ignore the fact that I am a fallible, physical creature, and bending my mind from its wandering to the confines of my heart, gut, bowels, breasts.

So I spend October groaning in an armchair by the fire, begging my husband in mousy tones to do the dishes. My stomach seizes up each time I open the fridge or cabinet: pregnancy heightens the sense of smell, and each whiff of old celery or leftover spaghetti is enough to summon a tide of disgust. Even the woodsy scent of the cabin's shelves and the gentle aloe vera in bodywash trigger an inner churning, as disorienting as trying to stand level on a pitching ship.

Unlike vomiting, headaches, or soreness, nausea is diffuse, more a malaise than a specific pain. It's not visible, it's not concentrated in one particular spot: it coils bitter and green through the body. It is one of the most difficult sensations to describe and imagine, and it is my initiation into a time in which words seem both terribly paltry, fake, and also as essential and sustaining as touch.

But nausea is only the misty backdrop to a cast of more precise, colorful pains. My breasts swell and ache. Coming down the cabin stairs, I clutch them like tumbling puppies. I've always had small breasts, the firm functional ones of an athlete, but in pregnancy they grow fat and lusty and unwieldy, wagging under T-shirts and pouring over the tops of bras. "How long is this going to last?"

Jorge asks, wide eyed. I give him a light smack and tell him they hurt like bruises, not to even think about squeezing them. In truth, he's intimidated by them and their new command of me, their blind, bursting, no-nonsense commitment to this mission that is taking me over in spite of myself. They are unbridled femininity, the first sign of a new and discomfiting softness.

My gut torques up, making room for the uterus. Most other organs follow suit, deferring to the growing womb, squeezing and contorting themselves to accommodate it. Even meager bowls of fruit inflict the horrible overstuffed feeling of late-night drunken bingeing. My belly balloons, not yet with baby but with gas and blockage. My blood sugar crashes an hour after I've eaten and, shaky, I devour handfuls of walnuts in an attempt to stabilize it. Headaches surge on the waves of increased blood flow and slam against the bones behind my eyes, over and over, all night. They recede slowly in the morning, leaving a hazy waste, a meek tiptoe into the next day, on the couch nursing coffee.

But of all the first-trimester symptoms, fatigue, which seems largely benign, is the one I struggle with the most. I am used to being out in the world: running, walking, sticking my head out the window of a Latin American taxi, dragging a begrudging boyfriend up the side of a craggy peak. But my body is now a tent that caves at the slightest gust. I try running on the road to the lake but make it no farther than a quarter mile before stumbling to a stop. I brace my palms on my knees, put my head between my legs, and weep. The valley shines with the finite fall bursts of copper and vermilion and gold and reinforces the fact that I am doubled over, shattered. Who is this person, and what is this life? Why did I want this? Every category into which I place myself—traveler, runner, tomboy, adventurer—seems to have paled behind the newly salient and oppressive designations of *mother* and *woman.*

Of course, I know these identities are not intrinsically opposed and should, in theory, overlap. The former, exterior me, the cocksure and outspoken one of certain opinions, knows that motherhood does not have to and should not overshadow one's self, career, or lifestyle.

But my first humbling discovery as a mother is just how constructed, precarious, and abstract my worldviews and beliefs are, how easily they may crumble in the heat of personal experience. In these earliest days of motherhood, before my baby has even grown fingers or toes, I sense that the labels I've long stuck to my life are only labels, that the hierarchies I've put in place—inside and outside, domestic and foreign, routine and adventure— are artificial and perhaps even cliché. Motherhood forces me to extricate myself from the sticky net of societal assumptions, from my own familiar ways of thinking and seeing, and, from the vantage point of a small homesteader's cabin in southeastern Ohio, take in the world anew: myself, my story, the way we build ourselves and stories and lives within the confines of culture and our own expectations.

What I cannot recognize at first, what I resist with that stubborn blindness we reserve for our deepest fears, is that perhaps I want the dramatic shift of motherhood; perhaps I don't want my life and myself to go on unchanged, motherhood like moving to another country and learning another language. Acquaintances of mine complain that everyone only wants to talk about their pregnancies, that they want to shout *I'm still me!* I want to counter *But I'm* not *still me* and *But I don't want to talk about anything else.* This feeling frustrates me; it seems to demonstrate new and surprising weakness. Me, of all people—so much her own person, such a champion of bold individualism—why can't I assert *still-me, still-me,* the birdsong of independent womanhood, and if I can't sing it now, will I ever again?

On that fall morning, while goldfinches flit in tidy arcs above purple thistles, I keel over on Kennonsburg Road and I fight. I wonder if a dogmatic biological clock has overrun my distinct life and personality, if I've been duped by hormones. I resist the exhaustion, the sensitivity, my rounded belly and breasts. I resist, above all, the softness of pregnancy. Pregnancy is all curves and couches and naps, all tenderness and susceptibility. I'd spent my twenties constructing a hard, certain self on the foundations of boldness, ambition, an ardent sense of justice, a lean and muscled body, and now pregnancy is a confusing tumble into uncertainty, interiority, quietness. I crumple on the road in the full fall sun and I sob, for my restless ego, for my decisions, for the sense of being terribly stuck, for the fear and hope of wrenching free from myself.

I fall into an intense depression, the first of my life. It happens quickly, like the air being released from a tire until what once was buoyant and strong is a limp snake-skin. The days are glorious, shining blue: the best of the year in Ohio. The pastures glow with goldenrod, the red maples dazzle the woods, crisp leaves twirl from on high into the creek, the sky blooms a deep pink at dusk. Dad and I discover a wild persimmon tree at the edge of the woods: so much ripe orange fruit, the size of an infant's fist, dangling in delicate ornamentation from each branch. In the afternoons I slump before the fire and weep. It is a scary, uncontrollable weeping, as if some force within is writhing itself out. I stop writing. I enter the liminal space of grief, where nothing that came before matters. The story I've been working on feels utterly irrelevant, its driving questions as flat and lacking in context as a practice conversation in a foreign-language textbook. My works in progress, these stolid pillars that had held up my life, that had seemed so essential and important, collapse and cease almost entirely to matter.

Yet for as bad as I feel, I'm not mourning the work. The distance I sense from it doesn't scare me; the fear comes from another, more obscure place, much deeper than concerns about success or productivity. In fact, the radical separation I experience from my body of work gives me an uncanny, unexpected hope: that when I begin writing again, it will flow from clarified, transformed seeing, from a frightening subterranean place I am being forced to acknowledge.

I spent the summer trying to figure out what type of writer I should be, operating under the assumption that if I could pin this down I'd have a clear winning strategy, and a way to dodge the fundamental uncertainty about why writing matters and why I do it. Now, having surged into a change so much bigger than the one I was expecting, where lives hang in the balance, I see clearly that all of this doesn't matter: whether I write fiction or nonfiction, novels or memoirs, whether I write at all. If I'm going to begin writing again on the other side of this, I will have to do so knowing none of it matters. This is one of a series of paradoxes I've wandered into in the confines of pregnancy, Ohio, this enigmatic homing: how to stop seeking meaning to find meaning, how to let go of myself to rediscover myself, how to not know in order to come into a different kind of knowing.

Relatives visit and talk with enthusiasm about the pregnancy. I feel as if I'm peering at everyone through a peephole, responding to their eager and oversize faces with muffled gestures from behind a wall. I want only to be alone. I wander with my dogs through the woods, crying tears as unstoppable as blood. Sometimes, I'm childishly angry; months ago, Jorge and I had lobbed around life options like badminton birdies. We could take off for Burma, we could travel around Africa, we could buy a Westfalia and cruise the desert Southwest. Neither of us really wanted any of these things: "Or," Jorge said, "we could just stay here at the cabin, through the winter, and read." This sounded lovely, but also puzzled and made me guilty. *I should be longing to explore the dusty back roads, should be searching for stories in the great beyond,* I reproached myself.

Now, I want nothing more than to go to Burma. Africa. The desert Southwest. Without the opportunity and desire to leap into the wider world at a moment's notice, I don't know who I am or want to be.

How much of myself is a core self, and how much is a reflection of the circumstances in which I choose to place myself, over and over, until they become motifs and myths? How much of myself have I created from the outside, with pride and fear, trying to adhere to an abstract ideal? How much of me is flimsy construction, how much bedrock?

Utterly unmoored, back in the land of the chirpy *hi* between the long *o*'s, I panic. Having confused travel with experience and experience with self-definition, I swing to a distraught conclusion: I am now doomed to stagnate in the domestic, the rooted, the body, the woman's realm of hearth and family.

In pregnancy I am forced to confront persistent cultural prejudices I've long held against the perceived feminine: against domesticity, motherhood, the imagined softness and weakness of introspection as compared with real, hard, muscular experience. I spent my twenties with men, challenging them to climb onto dubious watercraft and down another tequila shot. For years, I had only one or two female friends. I took this as a point of pride, as if the closer I hewed to the stereotypically male the more interesting and successful a person I'd be; an assumption borne out by many women writers, who receive the highest accolades and widest recognition when pandering, as the writer Claire Vaye Watkins puts it, to old white literary men. I have been devoted to the American religion of realizing my potential, my possibilities—and then creating more potential, more possibilities, in a perpetual froth of ambition.

I have absorbed the cultural definition of *settling* as an unfortunate compromise, particularly one made by a woman. There is an implied *for less* at the end of the term, with home, family, and rootedness comprising the *less:* less than intrepidness, less than rugged individualism, less than risk. To settle, to not push as hard and as far and as much as one can, to not roam, accumulate, and discover, is a particularly American defeat. It is to reconcile oneself to the here and now, the imperfect, the triumph of the banal over the exceptional, the inward turn as opposed to the outward gain, and as such has always seemed to me like a type of giving up.

But the primary definition of *settle* is to "resolve

or reach an agreement about." After years of looping around and around, seeking and finding and striking out again, I come to understand under an Ohio sky—trussed clouds, sweep of lavender, the vast horizon smudged with orange—the singular circularity of my search. *To settle: to turn one's attention to, apply oneself to.* To tread the same stretch of grasses through autumn, then winter; to memorize the low flapping of the horse fence, the rivulets that feed the creek, the butte across the valley that hoists the first signs of spring. *To become or make calmer or quieter.*

Only after moving back to the United States did I build up a strong cohort of women friends and colleagues and come to believe in the fundamental importance of a women's realm of shared struggle, stories, and ambitions. It has little or nothing to do with vapid pop culture depictions of rom-com girlfriendhood and can include wine and clothing swaps and boyfriend woes alongside critical readings of Adrienne Rich, manifestos, road trips in beat-up cars with a box of Cheez-Its wedged between the seats, the unafraid defense of one's writing before a skeptical crew of knowing men.

In the course of a few months, I went from zero female influence to running with a pack of women. These women had spent the past decade summiting Indonesian volcanoes and tagging birds in the Wyoming brush, and through this familiar entry point of travel and adventure I discovered a terrain of much-vaster shared experience, full of echoes and resonances I had never found with men. In these months and coming years, I also recognized that for as much as I may follow a male formula for success, traipsing through jungles and writing with cool detached bravado, I would never be afforded the privilege of maleness. If before I had been able to nurture a vision of myself as the odd one out, the prodigy, the foreigner, the strong woman running with men, I now came to understand there were forces I could never outrun, and that in the very act of running I was limiting myself and my writing to a narrow realm of proficiency.

Through the common experience these friends and I pored over, on Skype and in sad Brooklyn sublets and dank Pittsburgh bars, attempting to discern how we would shift from our twenties to our thirties, how our lives would change and narrow, how we would or would not hew to the traditional trajectories, I became passionate about the experiences of women and their representation in literature. I founded a magazine of writing by women and immersed myself in a growing literary movement that analyzed and denounced the way this writing is so often marginalized, trivialized, and ignored. I fought to reclaim what has long been defined as "female" as universal and challenged its depiction as frivolous or insipid compared to the "male" realm of war, exploits, and travels.

Yet in my own life the dichotomy persists: intellectually, I celebrate the interior and the rooted, but personally, even with a persistent sense of staleness, I cling to the exterior and footloose. For as much as I've come to pay attention to what it means to struggle as a woman in an overwhelmingly patriarchal world, to respect the connections that only women can share, and to recognize that I might find solidarity with women that I never will with men, I am still wary of being shoved off into some irrelevant, imaginary land of diaper bags and coffee dates.

Time slows, each day creeping along in infinite afternoons. At some point, in the clear light of midmorning, my hair still wet, I rush down to my parents' house, find my stepmom in the kitchen, and burst into tears. She guides me to the couch while I sob and explain that I don't know if I can or want to do this. Then she gives me what every woman deserves and needs: the respect and trust to make her own choices. She says, "We will support you no matter what you do." She says, Yes, this will change you. Yes, it will change your life. No, you might not be able to up and move to an island in the south Indian sea. But motherhood is one of the most elemental experiences in life, a transformation of consciousness. She says this plainly and honestly, as a lived observation and not an argument or a sentimental notion. She says it like setting a leaf on the table to be examined, its thin papery veins traced and studied. And she recommends Louise Erdrich's *The Blue Jay's Dance*.

I walk back to the cabin, breathe, order the book. I read it in the course of several days in front of the fire and in it find the initial nebulous answer to this period of grasping and struggling. It is the first book I've read in a long time that arouses a renewed vigor for living; that brings out the zigzaggy depth of the woods and the afternoon gleam on the creek; that has me, after a month of coercing myself to eat for sustenance, rolling a raspberry around on my tongue to taste the soft, sour dissolution of each segment. I've read dozens of books over the summer and early fall, spending whole Saturdays at a Pittsburgh park devouring *The Age of Innocence,* sitting on the cabin porch plowing through the eight-hundred fine-print pages of *Anna Karenina* after everyone else in my dorky classics book club bailed. But the pleasure most of these books gave was an intellectual one: I felt I should study the classics, and I thrilled at piecing out the components of sentences, scenes, plots. I didn't, however, connect with emotional resonance. I had forgotten that this resonance, the echoing of the book's bell long after reading, the quaver in the air of heightened perception, ultimately drives my faith in writing. Louise Erdrich reminds me of it without going much farther than a mile from her house. In *The Blue Jay's Dance,* she does not ride a camel across North Africa or wind up stranded in a remote Congolese village: she observes wild turkeys from her back porch and makes nests of her daughters' hair. She thinks. And the contours of her mind, as she eats nacho cheese, roams her backyard, and interprets the meanings of pregnancy, are enough. They grip, entrance, compel, as much as any adventure narrative.

One night not long after I finish the Erdrich, I go on a

walk through the woods and emerge in the back pasture. I hear a hoot, and stop, wait. Another low hoot echoes through the newly bare trees. Before, I would have kept on walking. I had things to do, places to be. But I keep waiting, watching the champagne-colored grasses bend with the wind. And moments later a different hoot, higher in pitch and crooked up at the end, rings from a tree or ridgetop to the west. Silence. Then a low hoot in response from the east. For maybe ten minutes, I listen to the owls calling to one another across the forest dusk. Steady, soft, haunted sounds.

I stand in the exact spot where, months earlier, I had sat in the damp grasses, smoked a cigarette, and thought, *What if I take a year just to become a better person?* It was summer, and the air was sweet and watery, the woods swimming in a twilight best described as midwestern marine. I'd just yelled at my dog in frustration and then, feeling guilty, marched off with what was left of the pack of cigarettes my little brother and I had split on our road trip. I was in the throes of a molting I couldn't quite name. I snuck my one cigarette at the pasture's edge, and in its clarity, all of my writing concerns, all my visions of success, faded. I thought of how few people get to dedicate a year of their lives to becoming better human beings. *Is that not enough? Is it not hard enough? What if that was all I aimed at for a whole year at the farm?* I lingered for a bit in the novelty of that thought, in the layered blues of a wet Ohio night. And then, when dark began pressing in from the woods, I brushed the smoke off my clothes. I hurried back through the pastures, the faintest whiff of dried leaf an undertone in the September night. I thought little of that moment in the happy bustle of the rest of the month, writing and drinking beer on the porch and hosting big dinners in the old red barn. And then I found out I was pregnant.

That same spot, where pasture meets woods, is where I listen to the owls. A few minutes after each hoot, I think to keep walking, but I wait. I wait until just beyond the point of satisfaction of curiosity and momentary interest. I wait until the moment has sunk in deeper, until it has pulled me out of the trajectory of my evening, until I have settled into it. I wait a little longer, and then, I walk on. And the next morning, I wake up, crack open a notebook, and start writing.

I write for hours. The farm is now gray and thick with winter. At nine weeks, I am in the full maelstrom of the first trimester. Occasionally I step outside to grab a rough log from the pile beside the door and throw it into the woodstove. The air is bracing, with the sandpaper roughness of winter. Inside, the cabin is dark. Two armchairs face the glow of the woodstove, and the two windows on either side of the living room let in a feeble winter light. My writing desk sits before the southern window, empty.

In the summer, I kept to a rigid writing schedule: a minimum of four hours a day, no interruptions. Four hours of total concentration and intensity, and then I'd be free. When it was over I would draw in a deep breath of relief and let it out. I'd droop over my desk, then stand and stretch in gratefulness.

But writing in my journal for the first time in years, the hours fly by without my noticing. I flex my wrist, check the time, and discover I've been writing nonstop for three hours. By hand. I fill pages and pages but never count them. A small connection sprouts between me and my baby, me and my pregnancy. I hadn't anticipated the intense loneliness of motherhood, the recurring sensation of living in quarantine from the rest of the world. It is akin only to the loneliness of grief, the way the colossal impact of loss grays the larger world into irrelevance. All the central dramas of life just months ago—will I get this book published, what kind of writer am I, should we live in the United States or Mexico—have disappeared, inconjurable, like love for a teenage ex-boyfriend. They have been replaced by the most mundane, immediate matters of the body—can I bear to chop this tofu? Is it okay to go running now or will I come back with the awful shakes?—and a need, baffling and enigmatic, for the big mysteries: God and family and death and love and self.

No one else can understand or fully enter this sphere: I inhabit it alone. Even my husband, with whom I share everything, cannot in the beginning cohabit the space of pregnancy. In this loneliness I thrash and resist and sink and then, writing through each cold gray morning, I rise. I buoy myself and discover another soul in this space with me. A nebulous, mysterious one, but an undeniable presence. This is not the cooing, precious, cuddly infant, the ubiquitous Baby idolized by mainstream pregnancy culture, but a human being, who in some ways takes care of me more than I take care of her.

One morning, Jorge and I wake to blue sky and a vista of gleaming white. The first snow of the season has blanketed the farm. We bundle up and traipse out with morning coffee in thermoses. The pastures and woods are held in that peculiar silence of snow, both heavy and light, hushed and expressive. In the woods the thorny tangles of multiflora rose have been bestowed an exquisite grace, shining in intricate patterns. The branches of the tall trees are burdened with a featherlight icing, crystalline against the blue. We crunch along, recognizing anew everything we've long taken as familiar: the dependable ash, their trunks tilting in gentle inclination with the hills; the tumbling ravine through which the dogs pound after deer; the creek. Around the abandoned house, on a hill to the northeast of the farm, Jorge saunters ahead to take photos and I stop. Gazing into the eastern trees, I see that their glazed branches have framed a perfect square of blue sky, a theater through which float silent clouds. For an unfelt stretch of time, I watch the snowy-white tufts drift across that ringing silence of blue.

I give up Burma, Africa, the desert Southwest, at least for the time being. For the first time, I recognize this delving into my own heart, mind, and body as a journey.

A voyage ranging sometimes no farther than the rounded softness of swollen breasts and growing belly, than a small cabin in winter warmed by a woodstove and smelling of wet dog, grass, and mud. And I acknowledge then what I've been battling and fearing all along: proof of my own ordinariness.

For so long, no one in my extended family had known how to treat me; my life and my choices refused recognizable frameworks. Now these people breathe a collective sigh of relief: I've fallen into step with a familiar pattern. They approach me, and over talk of nausea and contractions we connect for the first time. I've descended from some imagined terrain of the exceptional into which I've always placed myself, always sought to be placed, and become ordinary. And then I see that I have been ordinary all along.

How, I ask myself, can the most common of all human experiences be so overwhelming? How can it be so transformative and yet banal, so widespread and so unique? I've always associated the transformative, the unique, with being jarred out of commonness, out of familiarity. With being *out:* exterior. But now, in that worn blue armchair claimed by the mutt hound Little Dude, its velveteen fabric smothered in dog fur and smelling of forest musk, I range no farther than the centimeter thickness of the notebook and find transformation.

Maybe I've never trusted myself enough to sit still, to wait. Meaning lay in movement. Restlessness was energy, life. But pregnancy is nothing if not waiting. It is mulling for nine months in the dark, smoky hut of your body. The baby grows and incubates within you, and you grow and incubate within yourself. In this confined space—odorous, full of enigmatic throbbings and anxieties, adamant with the assertion of new life—you learn to slow down, to seek inward, to not do. To not apply, to not search, to not cast yourself into the future, to not strain for validation in exotic elsewheres and nexts and shoulds. To neither strive nor react. To wait.

In my dark cabin, moored by my mysterious body, I read. Isolated, completely and newly ignorant, I experience literature for the first time as vital in addition to pleasurable. I have always been skeptical of the claim that literature is imperative, redemptive, even lifesaving. Coming from a writer, I know this is potentially blasphemous. I grew up a voracious reader, my definition of *hedonism* a Saturday afternoon sprawled on the grass reading *Pilgrim at Tinker Creek*. But literature has always existed for me one or two levels above the raw core where we grieve, suffer, struggle to survive.

In pregnancy, however, I develop a craving for books not too distant in urgency from that for Haribo gummi raspberries. I read with a hunger and need I've never experienced, revisiting the birth scene in *Anna Karenina;* poring over Pattiann Rogers for hours on the porch for her scrupulous, unflinching wonder at gestation; consuming Anne Enright's *Making Babies* over the course of several evenings with the famished devotion of a disciple. I read viscerally, as if these books are in fact the retelling of my own experience. I discover, in other words, the universality of literature.

Whereas before I sought to differentiate myself, I now seek commonality; I am astounded by the fact that I can discuss, intimately, with real empathy, a shared bodily experience with Mexican market women and my aunts in Cincinnati and CEO friends in San Francisco. I start to see everyone as a baby. The man with a gray Santa Clausian beard and a T-shirt that reads BOOBIES MAKE ME SMILE at the Amish auction. The teenagers in their stiff turquoise prom dresses, sweating through zits and makeup. The immigrants mowing the measly strips of lawn on either side of the interstate. My parents. My editors.

Pregnancy has lowered me from this state of uniqueness I've long sought and shown me *you, too, are part of the most basic human experience*. But more important, it begins to show me that this ordinary experience, on a small patch of earth in Ohio, with aching breasts, feeling for tiny flutters in the belly, attuned to the slow passage of rain across the valley, is just as vital, insightful, essential, as the remote Chinese temple in mountain fog.

What if I take a year just to become a better person? But perhaps the quest isn't so much to become better as to allow myself to grow into the unknown. To let go of seeking and achieving. To let go of the notion that I am exceptional, and then to rediscover the exceptional in my own ordinariness.

This will be an inward year, a year of not doing, of waiting. And in many ways, it will be a year of failure. Failing and failing again and maybe, gradually, getting a little bit better at change, at growth. Each time I fail I learn more about the impossibility of living by any mantra or credo, of making a definitive pivot from one state of being to another. Each time I fail I sense the mille-feuille of past selves, givens, lives, wants, piled up beneath me, and I both resume and start anew.

On a brief trip to Cincinnati to visit my mom, she and I swing by Half Price Books. Mom, who has always liked dense philosophical and religious tracts, is browsing the religion section. Having scoured both nonfiction and parenting unsuccessfully for anything striking, I wander over to her. In one of those eerie, seemingly prophetic used-bookstore finds, I glance at the shelf on Buddhism and see Shunryu Suzuki's *Not Always So: Practicing the True Spirit of Zen* sticking out. The cover is a photo of his round ascetic face, small and polished as a nut, smiling that kind Zen smile that seems to dissolve all of my life's contortions into butter.

Mom buys it for me, then goes digging in her basement and gifts me her copy of *Zen Mind, Beginner's Mind,* heavily underlined and scrawled with marginalia like all of her old books. In this way Suzuki, a Zen monk and the founder of the first Buddhist monastery outside of Asia, becomes the accidental and divinely ordained guru of my pregnancy.

Suzuki writes, "After you have practiced for a while,

you will realize that it is not possible to make rapid, extraordinary progress. Even though you try very hard, the progress you make is always little by little. It is not like going out in a shower in which you know when you get wet. In a fog, you do not know you are getting wet, but as you keep walking you get wet little by little. If your mind has ideas of progress, you may say, 'Oh, this pace is terrible!' But actually it is not. When you get wet in a fog it is very difficult to dry yourself. So there is no need to worry about progress."

This change, this wrenching of self from self, is muddy and hard and painful, fought for through the thickets of consciousness and habit. There is no goal to be achieved, no adventure to be had: there is only a way of living, interior and distinct each day.

As the light wanes toward the New Year, the round swell of my belly in the bathwater grows bigger and more noticeable: softness firming into solidity. I begin to feel the baby move—first flutters and then rolls and, at times, the hard, unmistakable curve of bone against my skin. One night in December in the bath, I sense what it would be like to be in the womb, warm and quiet and cushioned. The line between inside and outside blurs, the baby in me and me in the water and both of us wet, warm, weightless. Lying on my back in that old claw-footed tub, looking up at the close wooden beams of the ceiling, my baby and I afloat in deep winter, I say my first prayer.

In early January, just around the time that the New

Year's resolutions start to go stale and all the uncertainty of another cycle comes flooding back, there is a polar vortex in Ohio. "A polar vortex?" I snort, when Jorge reads the weather from his computer. I think it might be an awkward Spanish translation. But then I check weather .com and, indeed, there it is, the polar vortex. For days, temperatures drop below zero; our pipes freeze in the middle of the night, which I discover only because I am getting up to pee every half hour. In a scene that would have strained credulity when Jorge and I met eight years ago in Oaxaca, he lies on his stomach under the cabin running a blow-dryer to unfreeze them, and succeeds. The creek solidifies into a creamy stream of thick ice; swirls of snowy wind pound the cabin at night. And then, abruptly, the vortex moves on.

Several days later, it is nearly fifty degrees, and the whole farm aches with thaw. I go running, and the ground is a sponge; my feet sink inches into dense, fragrant mud. Ferns and lycopodiums thrust their green from behind the thick padding of damp leaves, and the sky shifts abruptly between gray and a bright, fresh blue. Sun flashes in long swaths over the seeping and gushing woods like a diaphanous scarf trailed by clouds. The creek roars, the remainders of its hard ribbon of milky ice clinging to its banks, creating a slalom for the released waters. The world seems temporarily cracked free of a stillness, a containment, and it oozes and weeps and shines and shivers.

I ask Jorge to come with me to take the first photo of

my belly. I perch in the creek in my muck boots, imperfect, scared and tentative, excited and moved, looking up at the changing sky. I cradle the big white hill of my belly. I close my eyes. The day—muddy, wet, exuberant, frightening, uncertain, life forcing its way up through the ground and racing downstream over hard blue slate—is as good as any for conversion. I am on that precipice of transformation: I know this change is in me, I know I want it, and now I have to make it happen. And so I do what we humans do: I use the day as a marker, a new beginning. On this day, I say, a girl, a traveler, a writer, an adventurer, becomes a mother.

"Ready?" Jorge asks. I close my eyes, open them, study the shifting puzzle pieces of the clouds.

"Ready," I say.

MOTHERLAND

On our first night in Mexico, at the thirty-dollar-per-night Hotel Canada just off the Zócalo in Mexico City, Jorge dreams he's being chased by a giant gorilla.

"Subtle," I say. "Scared of something?"

I am twelve weeks pregnant. As predicted by my mother and sister, who experienced the same pregnancy timeline, the fog of the first trimester lifts. It is dramatic as a curve in the road and around the corner, clarity, sun, the smell of meat finally enticing instead of repulsive. It comes at just the right moment, when we land in a city of a million taquerías. I am surprised to find that I'm able to walk the streets for hours, attend a massive protest against Enrique Peña Nieto, stomach black beans *and* meat *and* jalapeños. I am, just in time for Oaxaca, ravenous.

Jorge has booked two weddings in Oaxaca. These

are paying for a monthlong trip to visit family and show them my still-tiny belly as proof that finally, finally, at the outlandishly old age of thirty-one, we are having a child. When Jorge called his mother to give her the news, her relieved delight boomed through his iPhone: *"Gracias a Dios!"*

Landing in Mexico reinforces the dramatic change of pregnancy. More than any other place I have lived or worked or traveled, Mexico is the country of my youth. In Mexico I fell in love, formed a close-knit crew of friends, witnessed a revolution, grew and changed and grappled with the dramas and decisions of my twenties. I am accountable to Mexico in ways I have never been to Peru or China or France or Japan. I have family there now, and community, and a history.

In Mexico I began to assert myself as a writer, and when I get really angry, when I yell about how fucked up the corruption or the machismo is, Jorge yells back, "Mexico *made you!*" As with all marital arguments, he is right in a piercing, painful way, and he is also exaggerating. My first big essays were all about Mexico; the piece about the goat slaughter in Huajuapan got me into graduate school and then into *Harper's*. Life in Mexico provided ethical, personal, romantic, and existential grist for my writing for years; Oaxaca was to me what New York City so often is to the aspiring American bohemian. And as such it is also the place I associate with singing in the street at four in the morning; with riding in the backs of pickup trucks through the cloud forest; with impassioned half-coherent conversations in scruffy cantinas about the nature of life. Mexico was the setting for the ambition and adventure of my late twenties, the place where carefree drifting began to channel into career.

Thus landing here with a baby in my belly heightens the sense of remove I feel from myself and my life. I see Mexico anew as both foreigner and—by dint of the tiny Mexican within—as something more. In Mexico City I am taken by the sensation that my baby has more claim to these dusky-rose skies and stone streets than I do; that within our small family I am the sole American, and thus my Americanness becomes more exceptional and definitive. At the same time, the baby's blood, swirling with the history of Zapotec and comal smoke and masa slapped between palms, makes Mexico mine in ways that transcend my life and self. I feel this already, at twelve weeks.

Jorge and I board the ADO for Oaxaca, as we have done time and again over the years. Usually I am giddy for the bus ride's vacillations between eager attention and withdrawn contemplation. I embrace the Ultimate Travel Writer Cliché and prop my Moleskine against the window, ready to note ads for freelance clowns and construct the perfect phallic metaphor for barrel cacti. But this time as the bus pulls out of the TAPO station, I feel detached, as if I am back in Ohio, rooted in the cabin and woods, and this shadow person is watching Mexico City jostle by outside her window. Or more precisely, as if some essential part of myself was left in Ohio long ago, has always been there, and I am just now becoming aware of her.

The volcanoes hulk in rare clarity in the distance, their snowcapped massifs regal above the confetti colors of this plain, and I am not myself-the-American noting the difference, or myself-the-American-married-to-the-Mexican, so much as a person entirely removed from it all, seeing the world via a gentle, fragile distance. I jot down images in my notebook, but not with the same fervor for accumulation and meaning making as in the past. I allow myself the wild abandon of a half package of Nescafé in a Styrofoam cup of hot water and just sit, absorbing details with the unfamiliar stillness of pregnancy. There a donkey hunched amid felled stalks of corn, there men with ragged shirttails working the fields, there uniformed schoolgirls disappearing down a dirt road, there people clumped under a sheet of corrugated tin, waiting for the bus. I know it so well at this point, and yet now that I have been shoved off the stage of my life, that I can't quite see or place myself any longer, I find I don't know it as well: there is so much I assumed I knew, I could describe with confidence contextually or historically or with firsthand evidence, but in this visit I sense the profound limitations of that knowing. More important becomes the process of putting aside what I think I know or can know to accept what I will never be able to understand.

We arrive in Oaxaca at night and climb the highway up the Cerro del Fortín until the whole valley is visible, a gleaming river of lights bordered by low black mountains. The memory of showing up this way when I was twenty-four years old, electrified by every strange scent and vision, hits me hard with that particular nostalgia of early pregnancy. Not only will Oaxaca never be foreign in this way again, but I have the intimation that it will be a long time before any place will feel so exotic, so new, so wide open to enthralled perception. The baby acts as a screen between me and the world; she is the ultimate newness, the ultimate exoticism, the ultimate discovery, and everything else pales behind her, everything else I experience predominately through her. The tightly spun cocoon of motherhood renders the world distant as stars, and yet at the same time its details become more intimate, more personal, part of a shared humanity that transcends context and borders. This is a paradox that Mexico highlights.

In Oaxaca we stay in a tiny studio in an old hacienda-style home that has been converted into a series of furnished apartments. Our place consists of a two-burner stove, a mini-fridge, a dinky shower, and a bed that eats up the majority of the room. On the roof is a tiled terrace with a view of the surrounding streets and jacaranda trees; doves brood on the scrambled telephone wires, and from the neighboring roof, inevitably, come the frantic yelps of a puppy chained in the sun all day long. It is the archetypal Oaxacan blend of suffering and tenderness, the beautiful and the crude.

It is also populated mostly by elderly Canadians and Americans who shuffle up the stairs shouting loudly, "Joe, there's a very nice show in the Zócalo tonight! Did you hear Mary came down with something? Maybe it was the ice!" They make us feel terribly young, like a couple in a short story who show up at an ancient farm-house, all fresh faced and innocent and preggers, only to confront a suspicious decrepitude. One man, somewhere in the haze of his fifties, alternately sits at a table on the patio or a table on the terrace drinking hard alcohol out of innocuous-looking cups. He reeks and talks too long and seems disconcerted when I reference my pregnancy, then opts to ignore it and offers us a drink. Supposedly he has a Mexican girlfriend, and in the day he disappears for hours to walk the colonias. Late at night I see his silhou-ette on the roof with a six-pack of Negra Modelo, pacing. Most of the other guests are corpulent, flowing-white-linen types, vocal and opinionated, accumulating various florid handicrafts. They are friendly enough but not terri-bly interested in us, which adds to my sense of invisibility and the feeling that I am carrying a secret. Their com-munity vibe—"Bill! Bill! Are you going to do the Zapotec weaving? The bus leaves at two-thirty!"—makes us feel like outsiders despite the fact that Jorge is from here, that I have lived and traveled here for nearly a decade. They lend to the overall aura of liminality and unreality, the sense that we have left behind our previous lives but not yet arrived at the new.

In the afternoons we have the best sex of our relationship. I am stunned that pregnancy has filled me with desire and set a million sensitive filaments I didn't know I had on high alert. Pregnancy sex feels both illicit and innocent, sex at its purest and also its most superfluous. This blend seems fitting in our situation, as we muffle our moans while heavy-sandaled elders patrol the hallways. We are at the core of layer after layer of secrets, hovering in this yellow-curtained room, in this small queen bed, in the heat of our intertwined bodies between what we were, what we seem, and what we will be. When it is over we lie side by side, listening to the whir of the fan, and then Jorge pounces up as he does and makes coffee and goes to work on his computer. I am slow, still, everything I do during this time in Mexico deliberate as if I might break a delicate understanding between me and this place, as if I need to move with the nearly invisible precision of an opening flower.

I sit on the rooftop terrace eating persimmons. They have the taut flesh of plums but the strangest most decadent interior of any fruit I've ever tasted. They seem as though they were crafted in an elaborate hipster San Francisco kitchen: a touch of Madagascar vanilla, a dash of Saigon cinnamon, and the plushness of a rum-drenched cake. We've never seen them in Oaxaca before, and we buy them in twos and threes at the market in spite of their exorbitant price. They appear only in my pregnancy; when we return over a year later we cannot find them anywhere.

I look out over the rooftops, bake my vulnerable body

in the sun, close my eyes. With them closed I can see Oaxaca as it has always been and always will be: the mountains like the raggedy coats of old horses, houses the color of soft dinner mints. In this city, in the past, I delighted in the blue hour, the time when the sky is drenched in a thick watery indigo and the hamburger stands turn on their solitary bulbs. As a traveler, so much of what I lived for was sensation, stimulation, the rare awareness that makes the most minute details salient. I craved the startling anecdote from the taxi driver; the dreamlike experience of wandering amid hundreds of goats herded by a taciturn twelve-year-old; the afternoon rainstorm narrowly dodged in a nook with fathers and schoolkids and aproned señoras. These experiences, and my capacity to notice and shape them, were the way I measured the meaning and vivacity of my life.

Now being in Oaxaca illuminates the fact that this type of noticing as a concerted act and sensory thrill has become superfluous, insufficient; I feel dulled to it, as if the old sensation tries to prick my skin and I register only the pressure. I am fully honed in on my baby and on my own interior landscape of change. My traveler's eye passes over the old man clutching a chicken piñata in the back of a pickup to focus on the subtlest shifts in my belly, the workings of memory and time, the new and tremendous solitude that sometimes steals my breath. It is not that I've ceased to care about the shifting kaleidoscope of the world outside or stopped engaging with it, but rather that for this stretch of pregnancy—and well into early motherhood—I give up on the passionate quest to understand and document it. I need to be inside my own body, my own heart and mind, sitting and waiting, sitting without expecting. "In my early years of sitting," wrote Buddhist priest and teacher Joan Halifax, "I tasted that stillness and knew that it was medicine."

Each time I try to conjure the active meaning making of my former outspoken adventurer self, my writer self on a quest to assemble the world into thematic overtures, I sense that I am missing an obscure, essential presence. There is work to be done and it must be done in this quiet space, with closed eyes that sense the mountains and sense the ironwork in the crumbling haciendas and sense the señora shuffling down the midday street with chiles rellenos nestled like puppies in the basket on her head, but with a concentration that stays in the interior. That waits out the urge to notice, the noticing itself, the gleam and shock of the world.

Sarah Manguso writes, "Writers must labor from a vague feeling, usually some large, old emotion, and in so laboring, come to understand the qualities of that feeling, and the source of it, and the reason they still feel it." I have long written with my eyes and my brain, twin tools of noticing, and in pregnancy these are no longer enough. I'm not able to explain what takes over from them, from what depths I am drawing my need and desire, until Manguso's definition illumes them like a lit match. I am living and struggling in these large old emotions of love and fear; they are literally in my gut, a way of being in the world that begins and circles back to the belly.

Little by little, I find that I can no longer be angry, or, rather, I can no longer trust my anger. I do not sense it as an integral part of me but watch it with distaste from the outside as if it were a disagreeable rash blooming and fading. On the terrace, bougainvillea and geraniums rain pink petals onto the tiles, the effervescent laughter of schoolkids rises from a nearby playground, the gas truck barks *"Gas de Oaxaca! Kilos exactos!"* Up here in the morning glare, I remember a bumper sticker from the nineties: IF YOU'RE NOT ANGRY, YOU'RE NOT PAYING ATTENTION. I can see it clearly on beat-up little Hondas making the trek from Cincy to Columbus. It might have had something to do with Ani DiFranco, or perhaps I just associate the two via the person of my best friend's older sister, a pale, outspoken vegan who introduced me to concepts like cruelty-free mascara. People like her, who knew what was done to bunnies in research labs around the nation and weren't afraid to show you in graphic brochures, made anger hip. They made it necessary, and young.

This notion of anger as a function of superior intelligence resonated immediately with me. I'd always had a razor-sharp sense of injustice that surely drove my parents to late-night, nerve-soothing gin. I was one of those kids for whom everything had to be equal, for whom the refrain *It's not fair* was the ultimate rebuke. This is, of course, essentially American: a naïve, frequently hypocritical obsession with fairness that is blind to history and context and the myriad complexities of a particular situation and instead bound to the rules of the preschool classroom. Righteous, precocious, and verbal, I was predisposed to inherit it in the worst kind of way. "Did you know," I'd say to my parents, my tone implying that *of course they didn't know because I was about to dramatically inform them,* "that the most educated people in the world don't have kids?" I let this fact resonate in the 1990 Toyota Tercel until it presumably rocked their worlds. I don't even want to imagine what I must have put them through when I read *A People's History of the United States* in AP History.

I spent a lot of time being angry in Mexico. Not all of this anger was unpleasant; much of it grew out of solidarity, community, deepening awareness. To share the anger at an inept government, at its blatant white-elephant construction projects marring the cityscape, at the murder and disappearance of activists, was a way to be woven more intimately into the tapestry of daily life in Oaxaca, to feel more connected to people and place. It was to form a united front and share a type of belonging and seeing. It was also the only form of empowerment, however illusory, we had against total impunity.

But much of the anger in these years was also miserable. There was the anger at the daily insult of harassment and the several times I was grabbed in the street; anger at bureaucrats who sucked up endless precious hours with their petty power; anger at the dysfunction and corruption palpable in pollution, strikes, protests. This type of anger bogged my life down in resentment, frustration, guilt: a suffocating moss of largely useless emotions. But not to feel anger seemed not only near impossible but also complacent, giving in to the inevitability of violent patriarchy and its everyday humiliations. To shrug, as many travelers I met throughout these years did, at "cultural differences" and adopt a paradoxically condescending distance from it all seemed a gross, smug privilege. And besides, I was not a traveler. I had a Mexican husband; I'd spent the better part of my postcollege life in Mexico. I framed the struggle with anger largely in these terms of cultural relativism. Either I saw Mexico as a colorful other whose problems were just part of an overall show of sometimes beautiful, sometimes dismaying difference I watched as an American, or I saw Mexico as my own and tackled the many indignities of life there.

Only now, in pregnancy, do I begin to see beyond this dichotomy to the larger question of my anger and its function. From the very beginning, the biggest surprise of pregnancy has been the sense that my seething emotional core—which could run from exuberance to outrage to abstract intellectual giddiness in an instant—has hollowed out entirely. In its wake is this disarming emptiness. To be empty has negative connotations in U.S. culture, in which being full, having more, having something rather than nothing to say, are heavily privileged; it would seem that this emptiness is a loss. But instead I feel freer. Not light, not airy, not unburdened of cares and worries, but less battered by the whims of my righteousness. More capable of seeing the way that anger is not necessarily an essential indicator of vitality but often a smug, shallow parody of it.

The opposite of anger is joy; the two emotions possess a parallel intensity, and neither lasts. Each is ultimately egoistic, shining its light on the triumph and exceptionalism of the bearer. I see now to the end of their fuses, the explosion and the fizzle and the what-next; I can't seem to get either to matter. It's not that I am bathed in the alleged beatific glow attributed to pregnant women, that I am suddenly taken with New Agey abstractions like respecting everyone's spirit and spreading loving-kindness (although I am increasingly skeptical of the hard shell of snark and irony that defines my generation). What compels me isn't so much the substitution of a new formula—balmy saccharine acceptance in lieu of anger—but rather that old profound place where neither matters. This is the place of birth and death, the night in the hospice with my grandmother, the moment I found out I was pregnant, when all of the opinions and surety of the everyday dissipate before an acute sense of the essential.

Pregnancy has the effect of setting me apart from myself, like pulling away a sheet of carbon paper to discover the outlines of my vulnerable and distinct personality vividly etched. *There is my fear, my insecure rectitude, an inner equanimity I've sensed but never quite witnessed, a need for control coursing bright red through my veins.* In demanding a total embodiment only experienced otherwise in extreme sport or meditation, pregnancy sets my tightly held self ashimmering as a constructed sheen.

There is opportunity here. My righteousness no longer appears a virtue but rather cheap insulation from complexity and uncertainty, creating surety but also walling me off from the potential for a deeper understanding of the type that goes beyond realizations and mantras and shoulds.

I first recognize this in a concrete way when I spot a Facebook post from a Oaxacan midwifery group declaring that vaccination is poisoning an entire generation. I am appalled. I plan on vaccinating my daughter, and the critical importance of vaccination has been highlighted for me via multiple posted warnings in U.S. airports about measles outbreaks. The baby could suffer grave and irreparable damage, or die, if I contract measles while pregnant, but the people responsible for the disease's resurgence in the United States don't seem to care about that. I am befuddled by a movement that seems so hostile to the well-being of communities in addition to individuals, and that so consistently refutes and distorts scientific fact.

The fact that Oaxaca's predominant organization of midwives, the face of natural birth in the city and one

of the only alternatives to ob-gyns, is spreading antivac-
cination propaganda is both depressing and infuriating. I
am disturbed that an organization I'd admired and pro-
moted to pregnant friends, an organization in charge of
the health of many women and children, not only could
be fearmongering with propagandistic generalizations
but could actually endanger public health, especially in a
place like Oaxaca with its high incidence of unvaccinated
street children and poor mothers at risk for disease. I start
to leave a comment on the group's Facebook page saying how disappointed I am, pointing out that this kind of
inflammatory rhetoric from blogs that distort scientific
fact—or flat-out invent conclusions—is dangerous, and
that it is particularly disconcerting to see it on the page of
a group dedicated to public health.

The old me would've done it without questioning, and
simmered the whole night with anger. *Of course* that part
of me thought, *this is wrong. It is just flat-out wrong, and
besides being wrong it is dangerous. I could write an entire out-
raged essay about this.*

Yet the old anger is dampened by sadness, or compassion, or uncertainty, or all swirled together. I think about
all the women I know in Oaxaca who've been forced
into C-sections that, in the United States, would've been
entirely unnecessary; the C-section rate in Oaxaca is
80 percent, while in most U.S. hospitals it hovers around
30 percent. Some women in Oaxaca have been told they'd
need C-sections because their babies weighed seven

pounds. There is a billboard above an ob-gyn's office near Parque El Llano, depicting the OB in scrubs, with a full medical team, standing over the body of a woman lying prone under white sheets; the OB is holding a screaming newborn upside down by his feet. In many ways hospital birth in Oaxaca resembles hospital birth in the 1950s United States: men aren't allowed in the delivery room, and women are told that if they move during labor their babies will die—my sister-in-law was told that if she stood up her baby would fall out and could be killed. On top of this, breastfeeding education is spotty at best; one nutritionist told an acquaintance to stop breastfeeding her premature baby at six months because the milk no longer contained any nutrients.

This organization, meanwhile, runs multiple support groups for pregnant women where all of these problems are discussed: unnecessary interventions, the medicalization of birth, the insulting way women are treated, obstetric violence, the myths and dehumanizing practices that make labor so much more difficult for women. The midwives focus on natural home birth and use many of the techniques that I want to use during my labor: movement, the presence of a strong support system including the husband, breathing, trusting the mother's instinct, not performing any interventions unless medically necessary. They also run a vibrant, thriving breastfeeding group that debunks so much of the widely perpetuated misinformation spread by doctors and pediatricians and challenges stigmas about breastfeeding in public.

And. But. Where do I stand, then? What does it mean to have a stance? What use, necessarily, does it have in this situation? Where does righteousness take me? To reject the group outright and despise them, and also to reject and despise the patriarchal OBs scaring women out of natural birth? All that I am left with is my own arrogance.

I begin to see that each of us carries a passel of fears like the heavy wicker baskets borne by Oaxacan señoras, woven handles slung taut around their foreheads. Some swear by the demonic powers of food additives; others would never let their children loose in a taxi; some loathe soap; others dirt; some heights; others meat.

My old anger is a solipsistic cycle of constant judgment, winnowing the world into a narrower and narrower sliver of acceptability until eventually all that is left is my own lonely, lofty rightness. To let go of it is not necessarily to dissolve in syrupy loving-kindness for, say, the grumpy old man who asks to switch tables when I begin breastfeeding, but to try to extend the gift of complexity to him and everyone whom in the past I might have treated as a pinned, motionless specimen, including myself.

Complexity is the hidden door in the wall, the blurted confession, the patchwork of irony furring our lives. It is the canned tuna I see piled up in a friend's kitchen. This particular friend is from a tiny village in the Sierra Norte, and he is a major critic of the United States and an advocate of natural, non-GMO, unprocessed fresh food. He loathes supermarkets and their packaging and advertising. He once held a birthday party in which the central dish was the spiny chayote squash that grows on his mom's property. He and his wife have a newborn baby, and we are at his house to celebrate. There, in the kitchen, stacked high with boxed milk straight from the supermarket, is the canned tuna, on which they have come to rely in the fervor of new parenthood. It is so incongruous I laugh. It echoes the image of another friend of ours, a cynical, sarcastic hipster from Mexico City who works as a curator, decked out in a feathered headdress, being bathed in ceremonial smoke during a Mexica wedding ceremony. Or my husband, the gentlest soul a tiny Mexican pueblo did birth, armed with a rifle in full camo in the rain on an Ohio winter morning. Instead of seeing these as anomalies, I begin to see them as entry points: the places where people become accessible, human, where we find empathy.

Of course, I still judge. Of course I think my decisions are the right ones, of course I take offense every day to injustices small and large. The difference is not the instinct but the aftermath: now, I reconsider. I step back; I make everything a little hazier, a little less certain. I turn the situation around and around like a Rubik's Cube, look at my own moments of weakness and strength. I bring in the *ands* and the *buts*. I hope that other mothers will do the same with me, although the impulse here is not so much altruistic as selfish; I want to save my own soul. I want to rescue myself from the isolation, the perpetual insecurity, of anger. I don't have to live in the deafening tunnel of my own assertions all the time. It is nicer out in the open, though quieter, more vulnerable.

This new sensitivity to complexity is tested by our trips to Guelatao to visit Jorge's parents. Rosa and Manuel are in their seventies, bent by age and slowness. A hardscrabble life of many children and never enough money has lumbered them with aches and pains, yet they persevere, tough as gnarled wood. They spend much of the day in their open-walled living room, taking in the near view of passersby and the far view of mountains grading into blue. Their relationship has not been without contention. Jorge's father had dozens of children with women in other villages. He was an alcoholic who frequently drank away his earnings and left the family broke. His mother worked making tortillas at the elementary school, and also did the laundry, the cleaning, the cooking, the waiting in line at the mill at 3:00 a.m. to grind corn. Their experience was not atypical in Oaxaca's Sierra Norte. In pictures from Jorge's childhood, his mother looks the same in many ways: already aged, already toughened by mountain sun and hardship, but radiating an innate kindness. Those pictures come from a reality of which I can barely conceive: young brown Jesuses in mock crucifixions on dry mountains, women in handwoven aprons carrying buckets, families walking through the woods in a wash of blinding yellow light.

Yet before pregnancy, this reality seemed more and more familiar. I assimilated it. It was normal to go to Guelatao on weekends for *memelas* and listen to la señora Rosa's stories of tiny elves making mischief in the early mornings, bread delivered by burro, the time Jorge got kicked out of church for singing *"Saca ese buey de la barranca!"* I went running on the dusty road between Guelatao and a neighboring village and collected pinecones with Jorge's aunts and uncles for the Christmas nativity scene. I knew this world in the way I knew Mexico, as a set of foreign experiences turned familiar, a thrilling reflection of my own worldliness.

But once the baby begins growing and the gap between me and what I thought I knew starts to open, the world where Jorge grew up and the world his parents still live in and represent becomes foreign in a new way. I listen to his mother relate her insatiable cravings to suck on rocks during pregnancy, a condition I now recognize as pica, indicative of malnutrition. I listen to her talk in the pragmatic way of many rural Mexican women of losing two children, and beneath her words for the first time I feel that deep black well of sadness that was as ever present and inevitable as the laundry heaped for her every day. I hear her describe giving birth to a little boy who had water coming out of his eyes and ears and died two days later. She had no time or space to grieve. Instead she had buckets of masa, her icons gathered in a dusky corner, little boys who wanted to paint Bart Simpson on her walls.

One child after another, nine in total, two dead and seven living. The last came when she was forty-eight years old and had hardly any money or time. Jorge was raised largely by an aunt while his parents worked.

For a while I struggle with thoughts I previously would have dismissed immediately as taboo, unsophisticated, and imperialistic. Although I know there was certainly no contraception available in pueblos twenty or thirty years ago (and in any case birth control would have been widely condemned by church and community), I still find myself thinking: *If there are so many mouths to feed and not enough to feed them, why another pregnancy, and another, and another?* I think now of my own child, vulnerable and utterly trusting, and feel a pang of sharp judgment, forgetting that childhood and the precious, protected innocence of children are relatively modern American inventions. I think of the moments I have glimpsed a raw pain and shame when Jorge talks about his childhood; I think of the stories he tells about saving up for months to buy basketball shoes or walking miles because he didn't have the twelve pesos for a taxi, and I am suddenly indignant at his suffering. I am more surprised by this anger than I am by any of Rosa or Jorge's stories, for I've heard similar ones many times. Now, though, they strike the nerve of a mother's ferocious protective instinct.

And. But. Jorge's mother grew up neglected by her own mother; an unwanted child, she was scolded and cast off for her dark skin, beaten for speaking Zapotec. She grew up in a society that brutalized the indigenous in much the same way the United States did Native Americans, segregating them, forbidding them the rights and resources of whites and mestizos both explicitly and implicitly. She grew up in a world where women had and still in many places have no power whatsoever, are impregnated from the moment they become fertile until they hit menopause, and can be thrown in jail for murder if suspected of an abortion. She grew up in a world in which men are largely unaccountable to their wives and families and are seen as whimsical as weather: alternately benevolent or dangerous, to be tolerated and appeased. How can I judge her?

Still, my anger resurges from a new maternal sensitivity. I remember the night not long after we moved in together when Jorge cried in front of me for the first time, recalling that as a child he was constantly afraid his roof would cave in. I feel misplaced anger at this woman, in many ways representative of women throughout millennia, who is at once a victim of violent patriarchy and a survivor, a loving and generous figure amid circumstances contrived to make her as small as possible. Jorge has tremendous respect for his mother. He remembers her pride and the sacrifices she made when he was growing up, as well as their suffering. Rosa tells me a story about how her own mother picked all the good plums from a plum tree and gifted them to Rosa's brother's children, whom she loved more than Rosa's; she then passed on the rotting and damaged ones from the ground to Rosa's babies.

Rosa gave them back; "My children don't eat leftovers," she said. Each time we leave her house, she foists as much as she can upon us: eggs, chayotes, apples, beans, sweet thick corn tortillas from a kitchen where she cooks over an open fire. She gives the little she has, as does Jorge, for he was raised in a world where the gift is sacred.

I, meanwhile, horde; I save, I accumulate. I will have one child and I will provide her with hand-carved wooden blocks and beautifully illustrated books and high-tops. And yet she will not know the dignity of a hungry woman who turns down a rotten plum because she knows her children deserve better; she will not know the scrappiness of curing strep throat with toasted rice and herbs, or have at the core of her soul the fatalistic conviction that we can only do what we can and no more. She will not know to put gravel in the road to hear *la carreta de la muerte,* and her heart will not leap when "Dios Nunca Muere" crackles from the village loudspeaker. She will not know what it means to give and give when she herself has nothing, to laugh in the most desperate circumstances, to cut off the feet of a baby's onesie so that he can keep using it even as he grows.

Each time we leave Guelatao, Rosa stands behind her sky-blue, waist-high iron fence and makes the sign of the cross. While I am pregnant, she makes it over my forehead and my belly, kissing the latter and resting her cheek against it, perhaps sensing that the baby inside will carry her name.

I know how to judge, and I know enough now to know

that judging is never enough. I see the gaping void behind each judgment, all it betrays and denies. I judge and then I must move beyond the judgment to consider all the convoluted nooks and crannies, longings and regrets, all the hidden resolves of Rosa's life, which intersects with mine in only the smallest slivers. On the other side of judgment is the world in its infinite complexity. The lemon trees that grow in a messy garden of broken pottery; Jorge's entire family gathered around the table for homemade pozole, each sibling with only two children, their hair polished and their feet squeezed into shiny leather shoes; the way Rosa laughs when the babies tear and scatter the petals of her beloved fuchsia; the coffee and conversation and *que dios le bendiga* offered each of many casual visitors to the patio, their camaraderie amid the sierra's caprices of heat and cold.

Late one night in Guelatao, crammed in the tiny smoky kitchen with Jorge's parents, his sister and brother-in-law, and their two teenage kids, I confess a sugar craving. We've just stuffed ourselves with *memelas,* thick corn tortillas that Rosa has rolled by hand, toasted on the comal, and topped with homemade black beans, salsas, and *queso fresco,* and now I am lusting after dessert. At fourteen weeks I am a black hole that absorbs insane quantities of food and is never full.

Before pregnancy, I had no sweet tooth. I've always been a cheese and chip person, much more liable to make a late-night grocery run for Sour Cream & Onion Pringles than doughnuts. Cheez-Its fueled my last-minute lit papers in graduate school. But, newly pregnant, I beseech Jorge to hop in the Honda and drive ten minutes to Dandy Don's for raspberry pie. Rural Ohio yields happily to my cravings, offering up five-pound pies in every shade from peanut butter to lemon cream, deep-fried long johns coated in maple icing, apple fritters, buckeyes, soft-serve dipped in toffee and drizzled with caramel. Mexico is trickier.

"Pastel, dónde podemos conseguir pastel?" Adi, Jorge's sister, asks Rosa. I sense a mission forming and quickly back off, saying, *"No, no, está bien, está bien,"* not wanting to be high maintenance. But Adi is already calling their sister Bivi, not once but twice and then three times until she gets through. Bivi is en route to Oaxaca with her husband and two daughters, the lot of them stopped at an *elote* stand eating roasted corn drenched with mayonnaise, lime, and cheese, when they get the call. They turn around, and Bivi runs back upstairs for a piece of strawberry-peach cake stashed in a Tupperware in the fridge. This cake makes the winding night journey over the mountains and is handed triumphantly to me when the family arrives. The kitchen is filled to capacity with bodies bustling in the smoke and glow. We all kiss one another on the cheeks, Rosa starts a new round of *memelas,* and I devour the *pastel.*

Sugar, I think, sugar passed from woman to woman to woman to my baby, the sweetness of generosity that transcends all judgment, and which I have found in Mexico more than any other place in the world. I think of the blind singer on the bus with his deep, resonant voice, swaying down the aisle, and how as he sang people dropped two or five or ten pesos into the can he was clutching, then reached out without thought or hesitation to still him as the bus lurched. Joan Halifax writes, "This is where God appears; not within an individual, but between beings."

On the twelfth of December, the day of the Virgen de Guadalupe, I feel my uterus for the first time. Jorge and I are lying in bed in late morning, and I am running my hand over my belly as I do now, trying to discern the mystery within. What is that lump just above my pelvis, just below my stomach? At the end of the path of soft hairs that descends from my belly button is a ledge. It extends a good length across my lower abdomen. I trace my hand across it, press it gently, and realize from all my avid BabyCenter reading that this is it, the uterus, in its gradual rise toward and over the belly button and nearly to my breasts, edging out all other organs in its supremacy. The knowledge that this is it and it is growing and it is big enough now at fourteen weeks to feel with my hands makes me absolutely giddy for the first time since I found out I was pregnant. "I can feel my uterus!" I announce to Jorge as though I've won a massive stuffed animal at the fair, and Jorge, steady as he is with these pregnancy ups and downs, gives it a quick rub and says, *"Órale!"* then jumps up to make coffee.

From outside comes the faint blurt of bands playing for the Virgen. In Parque El Llano, hundreds of people are pressed into small booths that replicate imagined landscapes of Bethlehem, with waterfalls of shiny blue foil and waxy palms and sand strewn on the old stone, and before these landscapes stand donkeys, horses, beasts of burden (some real and some fake) on which people poise their small children. The boys, even the tiniest babies, wear the traditional buff-colored linen garb of peasants, hats onto which the image of the Virgin has been sewn or pinned, and serapes that feature Guadalupe aglitter in red, white, and green. Girls wear embroidered dresses and bright twin braids woven with ribbons. Their parents will press into the Templo de Nuestra Señora de Guadalupe in a slow-moving mass that inches toward the priest, who douses his hands in holy water and splashes the crowd in a broad arc. Some, lightly spritzed, will push back for a moment more to coat their faces. They emerge dripping into the blinding sun. Babies are stunned. Outside, women sit in a long line beneath the palms and nurse. Cripples beg at the church entrance, bananas fry in huge sizzling vats, young men hidden in hot, enormous priest costumes joke with passersby.

Meanwhile, a half-dozen blocks to the south, I lie in bed and listen to the distant tinny blare of the brass bands, rubbing my uterus as if in greeting. I wonder if the baby is absorbing this via osmosis, if the motherland bestows a series of enzymes on its children, a longing for a particular type of air and light, an intuitive map of sensations that can be written over but never truly erased. I think of waking to the shock of snow, of that pale purple light at dusk and the smoke threading from chimneys, winter mostly, what sets Ohio apart from nearly all the other places I have lived. I think of Jorge and his diabolic grin over a plate of *enfrijoladas con tasajo,* the way he says *"Mira!"* like a child as we drive through the Sierra, its ridges running piney and blue as far as we can see. I think of the way he changes in Oaxaca, his musculature loosened, his bearing open, a new guilelessness and joy gentling him. He is already a kind, sweet soul in Ohio, but in Mexico he blends with the landscape, the people, loves them in a way that makes me jealous. I lose part of him as Mexico absorbs him. This has long been a source of tension in our relationship. When we have our big fights, the bad ones about the huge looming questions of where and how to live, Jorge comes back to the same insult: "You have no home," he seethes. "You're just jealous because you have no *tierra* of your own." For a long time, he is right. I pride myself in a distinctly *estadounidense* way on not belonging anywhere. I am not so much a citizen of the world as I am unaccountable to any place and able to freely critique or embrace them all. *I love Japan,* I say, or *The food in Mexico is unbeatable.* But as I carry my baby through the Ohio seasons, from the luminescence and fade of fall to the first bite of winter and the freeze of the creek, as I carry her into the pale spring and then the riot of summer with its crush of humid leaf and smell of sassafras, I am reborn in Ohio. I remember what has always been present but what I have forgotten or neglected: this place is in my blood. Not only the stolid midwestern German refusal to spend $1.79 on a muffin and the predilection for practical rain gear, but the dirt, the rot, the flower, the rain, the wood. I lug bits of maple and white pine and clover on planes around the world to islands and tropics and Patagonian mountains. In Mexico my blood stirs with this awareness, my baby newly palpable in the fastness between belly button and pelvis, Ohio newly palpable in my veins and skin and eyes.

Many of Jorge's and my fights have stemmed from the way he defends Mexico like a rattler coiled before its lair. I grow exasperated and he lashes out, tells me to stop whining or to show some respect for the fact that here we can hang out all day drinking fresh-squeezed orange juice under the laurels, that here life is immediate and urgent and felt. Jorge embodies Mexico, its wounds are his, its beauties his triumph and heart. I have never conceived of Ohio in terms of wounds or beauty, and for a long time I have hardly seen it as a place. Instead it is a backdrop, of cheddar cheese and jungle gyms, Trivial Pursuit and loading the dishwasher. Jorge has the gift of a motherland: his smoky house, the comal atop the charred wood, the mountains spilling in every direction under their perfume of mist.

In pregnancy, when the alchemy of making new life is constantly on my mind, I discover Ohio as my own motherland. It still sounds ridiculous to me, everyone still laughs when our friend Eleutario asks, *"Sarita, cuando te vas a tu tierra, a tu ranchito?"* with the ironic implication being that the United States is nobody's *tierra* or *ranchito* but an antiseptic modern opportunityscape of work and money. This, too, is true; I realize it in the air-conditioned vastnesses of Target and the streets emptied of people. But place is made by perception as much as environment or exceptionality. Ohio is a place if I make it one in ritual, attention, and affection. I glimpse my childhood self in the woods, playing in the shroud of trees. I think of talking on the phone to my mom in the cabin's small kitchen, eating Grape-Nuts.

"Mmmm, Grape-Nuts," Mom says. "Do you let them get a little soggy in the milk?"

"Of course," I say.

When I return, I will make a scrapbook of Grandma Menkedick's recipes, with entire pages devoted to cheese balls and coleslaws and desserts involving pretzels and cream cheese. This is the baby's, too, along with the jacarandas in blossom in the fog.

I recognize now that place lurks in us like a gene waiting to be expressed; we may repress it, or we may turn it on full blast, but regardless it is always there. I think of a man I saw once when Jorge and I went to watch the Semana Santa rituals in Tlalixtac, a village outside of Oaxaca. Easter in Oaxaca is not fields of giggling children collecting pastel eggs; rather, it is men in full Roman regalia whipping—literally whipping—a live representation of Jesus who drags a 120-pound cross. The Jesus wears a crown of thorns, is actually crucified (though he is tied to the cross, not nailed), and is barely able to limp back home after the re-created Passion. Young men wait years to play the role.

Jorge and I followed the procession to different stations staging moments of Jesus's trials, and at each one a man in a cheap purple polo and the pointy-tipped black boots worn by rural workers blasted mournful notes on his trumpet into the quietly rustling crowds. It was more than ninety degrees, with hundreds of people clumped in sweating masses on the sidewalks, their umbrellas in staggered layers over their heads, and this dark-faced man held forth with the self-possessed, innate composure of a believer. Like so many other people I have observed in Oaxaca, in ritual and fiesta, he embodied his role, blended and disappeared into it.

I think of him when one day, walking the streets, I see a Virgin on a float during a parade. She is the best Virgin I have ever seen, the one I'll always remember. She could be twelve, fifteen at max. Her eyes are the jade green of sea glass. They look over the revelers unmoving, unseeing, ethereal. She is neither fragile nor strong. She is in the way mountains are, or myths, or dreams, haunting, looming, more real than the real. Her features are plain, neither strongly indigenous nor Hispanic, without distinguishing marks. An angel offers her a *torta:* "Ten." She shakes her head slightly without shifting her gaze. The angels sip small plastic cups of *agua de jamaica*. A band blares the standards; tourists duck *dulces* and grin from the sidelines with their cameras. *Las chinas oaxaqueñas* dance with their broad white grins, lifting their dresses into wings of silken candy pink. Five p.m., the traffic pants at corners, held back by the palm of a transit cop. The Virgin, green eyed, lips still, without expression, takes no note of me or anyone, aloft and shrouded in her blue satin. The parade stops for *las chinas* to dance and *mezcal* to be poured, and la Virgen stares on unseeing, forever and ever.

I have seen many incarnations of the Virgin—this is Mexico, after all—but all have been aware of the tension and rift between themselves and their role; they could not, or did not, blur with it. We all carry the potential to disappear into such a role: maybe not the young Virgin Mary or the crucified Jesus, but a taciturn grandmother or an angry father or a tactless yokel or a folksy liberal in the New Mexico desert. Some people fearlessly embrace their roles, as legacy or destiny or comfort, and others reject theirs with distance and silence, but regardless, the role remains, like a snow angel in precisely our shape, just waiting for us to lie down and fill it.

Before we leave, we spend another night and day in Mexico City, as we often do to bookend our trips, since flights from there are far cheaper than those leaving Oaxaca. I am now nearly sixteen weeks along, and the month

I have spent here devouring tacos and *tortas* and tamales has culminated in sensational heartburn, which will dog me into the third trimester. I have taken to swallowing a half cup of apple cider vinegar, pure, to ease the flames. Still, heartburn is preferable to the perpetual unease of nausea, and supposedly means that the baby will be born with a full head of hair.

On our last night we walk the pedestrian streets of central Mexico City, through the cacophony of the impending Christmas vacation. Musicians croon and strum guitars under the eaves, pedestrians idle in throngs, clouds of meaty smoke rise from ubiquitous taquerías and interwoven into it all is the insistent droning of *ambulantes,* selling everything from pralines to polyester vests to glow sticks. *Diez pesitos llévale llévale diez pesitos llévale llévale diez pesitos* goes the monkish chant, over and over. One guy, older, slightly frazzled, in a plaid shirt and jeans and white sneakers, is making a tiny skeleton dance in the midst of a growing circle of intrigued passersby. The skeleton isn't more than an inch high, the cheapest flimsiest bauble of plastic. Still it dances like the most liberated reveler in one of José Guadalupe Posada's postmortem fiestas. *"Siéntate,"* the man says, and the skeleton sits. *"Párate,"* he says, and it stands. Then, "Boom!" and the man shoots it with his finger, upon which it crumples, motionless. The crowd gasps. Soon it's up again to join another skeleton, also maneuvered by the man, which it kisses. *"Beso!"* the man says, and the *beso* leads to the two skeletons collapsing in amorous fever and frolicking on the cobblestones. There are Christmas lights on the colonial buildings, a huge warm circle around the minuscule figures. Jorge caves and buys one for *diez pesitos,* and I laugh at him, chide him, *Sucker, sucker.* We lose it that very night in the jumble of our possessions packed and unpacked.

The next morning we eat breakfast at El Popular, the diner we visit every time we're in town, with transcendent *café con leche* and decent chilaquiles. Afterward Jorge returns to the hotel to finish packing, and I take a quick walk to the Zócalo. The next time we're in Mexico, I think, I will be a mother.

On a whim I enter the cathedral at the Zócalo's north side, built on top of an ancient Aztec temple. I haven't been in here since I first came to Mexico nearly ten years ago. It is cavernous, echoing, and solemn. I walk slowly, looking up, taking in the weighted silence. Just before the wooden fence that prevents tourists from entering the area of pews and the altar, there is a visitors' book, where people leave comments and prayers. I pick up the pen. I write of my love for Mexico, of the years I have spent here, of my baby growing up between worlds, and then I pray for her on that thin frail paper in this great hall, this temple upon a temple. My hot breath catches in my throat, the tears obscure my writing. Then I breathe, set the pen down, make my way back toward the light.

Mexican writer Elena Poniatowska wonders, "How

much of me there is in these faces that don't know me and that I don't know, how much of me in the subway, in the steps that pile up, one on top of the other, until they finally come out into the great, white spout of light, how much of me in the last, weary steps coming out, how much of me in the rain that forms puddles on the pavement, how much of me in the smell of wet wool, how much of me in the rusted steel sheets, how much of me in the Colonia del Valle–Coyoacán buses that rush along until they crash and form part of the cosmos, in the graffiti on the walls, in the pavement, in the earth trod on a thousand times. How much of me in those worn-out benches, their paint flaking, how much in the hardware stores, in the little corner stores, how much in all those testosterone shots on those dusty pharmacy shelves, in those syringes that used to be boiled and that spread hepatitis, how much of me in the signs that used to hang all along San Juan de Letrán: 'All types of venereal diseases treated,' how much in the newspaper stands, in the Fountain of the Little Frogs, in the shoe-shine boxes, in the rickety trees—just like little sticks climbing up to the sky—in the man who sold electric shocks, in the old people's wrinkles, in the young people's legs."

If our baby is a girl, I will name her Elena.

When we arrive at the farm, the afternoon is clear blue-gold, and soon the woods are red with winter dusk. The evening light turns the creek to a ruffled gown. I sit on the bank and feel a bodily relief, an old feeling—long forgotten beneath all the complex layers of adult love and sex—which returns now in pregnancy. It is the relief of the infant picked up and soothed, of the child who collapses into her parent's arms after she's fallen. It is the comfort of the elemental space of mother-baby, before the baby pulls away to form an independent self. It is the belly, the soft hill of the shoulder, the nook between collarbone and neck, the nipple, the gently rising-falling pillow of the chest. It is attachment to a larger body that eclipses and absorbs one's own, and this is how I feel now when I hug my mother and need her bodily as I haven't in years, need the reassurance of her arms enclosing my helplessness, and it is how I feel at the farm on this carmine dusk, when my stretching body eases onto the leaves, when my eyes trace the insinuations of the stream, when the beeches and the oaks that form a canopy over the water take my scampering mind from me and sync my breath to the fading day.

A WILDERNESS OF WAITING

IN THE SEEMINGLY INTERMINABLE MIDDLE of my nine-month human pregnancy, I go on a Googling binge of animal gestation periods. Frilled sharks, I discover, gestate for forty-two months. Elephants take twenty-two. Sperm whales: sixteen. Walruses: fifteen. Rhinos: fourteen. Horses: eleven. I am seeking solidarity and comparative comfort in the realm of beasts, seeking to place my experience on a spectrum of waiting. I think of going on into month eleven, twelve, twenty, thirty-five: days into months into years of pregnancy. I find a kind of horror in it, and fascination, and reverence, and ultimately a question: What does it mean to wait so long that the line between life and waiting blurs?

I've always hated waiting. I am that person craning her neck out the window in traffic to see as far ahead as she can; the one peeking over shoulders in the coffee-shop line, trying to determine why it's taking so long to get to the counter. I come to bus rides and plane trips equipped with a dozen novels, magazines, sketchbooks, notebooks, podcasts, and playlists. I can recite in wearisome and alarming detail every moment of my day, arranged into a checklist of tasks judged successes or failures by their degree of necessity and productivity.

Like most people, I also have systems both elaborate and simple for carving up days, weeks, and months into comprehensible and wieldy increments. In the quotidian, there is the morning coffee, for the initial writing spurt and gearing up for running, and then the whole afternoon tilts toward that early evening beer, after which the day begins its final descent into dinner and a nighttime of Indian takeout and *Mad Men*. To appease a larger restlessness, there is the anticipation of the end of academic semesters, the summer, trips home or abroad, the return to school, the granting or not granting of fellowships, the publication or rejection of stories: imagined futures like bobbers on a lake, watched with shivery expectation. I am perpetually casting, breaking up the monotony of the landscape of time with teetering red globes on the verge of abrupt submersion. And in the meantime, there are the daily markers and escapes of routine and substances.

But pregnancy is characterized by a total physical and psychological immersion in the present and the body. In its months-long middle, in particular, the web of gestation is spun so tight that the past becomes inaccessible, so remote as to belong to another person's life. The future is equally impossible to conjure: how can one imagine the brand-new human built from scratch, the meteoric impact of her arrival? The boundaries of the world shrink to the parentheses of the belly.

At first, I felt all of this frustrating temporal impotence mostly in terms of beer. A cold brewski, it turns out, was one small but crucial element in my daily domination of time. I work from home, and not having that clear pivot point between work and leisure threw the whole day into interminable monotony. It was as though, without that reward and demarcation, it almost wasn't worth working at all, or rather when and how I worked became irrelevant if the whole day was a soup with no beginning or end, no anticipation or release, sloshing into the soup of the next day and on and on.

In the brutally slow final months of 2014, my dad lends me *The Places That Scare You,* by Buddhist nun Pema Chödrön. Chödrön counsels about the many ways we find escape in our days—sex, TV, booze, food, drugs, exercise—and warns how hard it is to let go of these crutches, which attempt to mask what for me became apparent in pregnancy: the fact that time is a crushing monotony, so much vaster than us and as unconcerned as the moon with the ways we attempt to dominate it. Our tricks, our counting down of days and meting out of recompenses, our constant rigging of bobbers to watch, mask the fact that we are always changing and yet not changing at all, and all of our elaborate performances of success and failure, productivity and lethargy, are ultimately, to paraphrase Chödrön's teacher Chögyam Trungpa, so much makeup on space.

It is easy to be fooled by the trick of the pregnancy calendar. At first, it seems pregnancy is the most tantalizing bobber of all. There are so many ways to mark the passage of gestation—months for the laid-back, weeks for the anal, and days for the truly OCD. There are pregnancy books that inform expectant mothers of what is happening in the womb each and every day of pregnancy: *At twenty-two weeks, five days, the baby is now covered in tiny fine hairs called lanugo.* It seems therefore that gestation would provide the ultimate illusion of control, the ultimate beginning, middle, and end.

And yet all of these markers come to seem a flimsy linear story grafted onto a truth that defies narrative. I read through all nine months in *What to Expect When You're Expecting,* first all at once and then individually as I near each one, and each week I go to BabyCenter.com to see what the baby is up to—growing fingernails, opening its eyes for the first time—but still I do not feel time passing in the same way I did before. The weeks and months do not feel like a progression, an arrow or a line, as much as they do a space I have entered and am inhabiting. Time as a bowl, with me nestled at the concave bottom, the days and weeks orbiting around me, no clear forward, no back.

• • •

Sometime after Thanksgiving my niece and nephew visit. We go on a hike: through the maple woods to the east of the cabin, down near the pastures, then back into the far woods along the creek, returning via the old township road. This is the route I will follow nearly every day for nine months. Inspired by Louise Erdrich's *The Blue Jay's Dance* and hungry for symbolism, I hunt for bird's nests. I find three, their thin bark fibers wound tight around the wishbones of young branches. Some are tidy as a ballerina's bun, and others are messy with dried mud walls and haphazard leaves overlapping. My niece and nephew walk atop fallen logs with the careful steps of gymnasts, their arms outstretched. They clamber through a small tongue-shaped ravine, stirring up torrents of leaves and lunging themselves forward on vines. I feel almost ghostly beside their vivid presence, my body a slow-moving woodland creature, the nests featherlight in my hands. These raggedy-haired kids consume time wholly and enthusiastically without thinking, the way they gulp lemonade. I feel unhinged by it, uneasy.

In the smoky fall evenings, I walk the pastures, slowly; in the past I have been that person on the sidewalk rushing around the dawdlers, the one who soars past all the other airline passengers and is through customs by the time they're beginning to bunch up in line. Now the dogs race to the end of the pastures and come pounding back before I've crested the hill. They stir up flocks of wild turkeys, who hurry through the grasses in their balls-out scramble, then lift into improbable flight over the woods.

On longer walks the dogs and I wind our way through beech forest to the top of the ridge, where the winter sun breaks through clouds and illumes a grand oak with a mockingbird in its top branches. The ridge is a palette of Ohio winter colors: storm and wheat, navy and honey, ice and yolk. An old road, long overgrown, runs along the ridgetop. Breezes, not yet bracing, stir the dried sumac and the grandfatherly pines.

At night, I hear the faint booms of my heart when I lay my head on the pillow. By now, twenty and then twenty-four and then twenty-eight weeks into the pregnancy, my blood volume has increased by almost 50 percent. My organs are squished, my ligaments stretch and ache. My mind is rooted deep in my body, and both are rooted deep in the here and now. The past and future fall away, and I am steeped in a fog that is the present and also beneath it, beyond it: the time of birth and death. My body has become a different kind of space, at once turbulent and surreally calm.

On one level, an upper level, there is distraction and detachment, like what I've often felt on my period: biological fervor preventing a clarity of thought and focus. I have completely lost my ability to make small talk. I can't dredge up witty anecdotes from my day or recall

all the peppy questions that keep conversation alight. As an extrovert, I find this frustrating and distressing. But beneath the surface distraction is the quiet of a river or plain. An interior wilderness of waiting, and when I allow myself to descend there and inhabit it, to wander timeless without path or purpose, I discover an unfamiliar way of being: connected neither to past nor future nor the sensory now of moments but to the huge, quiet, endless flow of time.

Jorge and I sit on the porch one evening trying to make conversation. I think we should talk about writing and photography, about the meaning of art or the portrayal of marriage in *The Americans,* but I don't really feel like talking about any of these things. Jorge's responses are halfhearted, and the conversation sputters, stalls. I am still disarmed by my lack of desire to talk, to think, to spin the world into intellectual cotton candy. There is a lull. In it Jorge stands and lunges at our mutt hound Little Dude, who makes a comic leap some five feet back and bolts around the yard in a cartoonish streak. He chases her in circles. "Leeeeetle Duuuuuude!" he shouts like a Disney villain. He returns, sits, panting, and I scratch the now-wary Little Dude under the chin. Jorge takes two glass bottles from a box of twenty we bought for two dollars at an Amish auction, holds them in the wind so they whistle and sing. Their pitch rises, pierces, and I tell him to stop. He looks at me petulantly.

"The one thing I don't like about you is that you don't

let me make my noises," he says, and it is so ridiculous and precious that I laugh. "Go on then," I say. "Make your noises." He cups his hands together to make a rising bird-like call he says he learned in his village. The Jorge whoop, echoing over the porch, the pastures. The moon is a deep-violet circle, one small sliver of which is illumed bone white. It inches northward through the bare branches of the walnuts, a little higher each time I look.

One late afternoon in January, I sit on a rock above the creek, watching my dogs sniff around the dried leaves for rabbits. I try to sculpt the afternoon into part of a story, a scene, but I can't think of anything at all, not even of being where I am—the glassy water falling over slate, the rustling of dog paws, the absorbing silence of moss. All I can do is feel the vessel of my body, my consciousness drifting in and out of it like mist.

This is pregnancy as, alternately, Zen state or acid trip. Zen state when I allow myself to see this strange wilderness as calm, spiritual, comforting, and acid trip when a restless frightening energy pulses behind it. In the latter case, I feel trapped by hormones, irritation and boredom threatening to overrun the precarious witnessing of what Suzuki calls "things as they are." I want to come down off this hormonal high, to be released back into time and straightforward thinking. I want plans and progress. I chafe at this stillness, this inability to be anywhere but a small cabin in middle-of-nowhere Ohio.

But then I am boiling eggs in the kitchen, in my socks,

and I am laughing a belly laugh that is new since I got pregnant. It is a laugh with no inclinations other than happiness, both full and empty. It is a laugh surprised at itself. In the close light of the kitchen at night, I am watching the water bubble around the jiggling eggs, feeling my husband nearby on the couch. All of my life flies by in a glimpse of irrelevant time and returns to this.

One morning Dad comes traipsing up to the cabin in his camo muck boots. He knocks, the dogs bark, I put the shepherd in her kennel. In his hands is a dead bird, brown with white streaks along the sides. "It's a rufous-sided towhee," he says. "You hear them when you go turkey hunting. Isn't it beautiful?" We stand for a few minutes to admire the frozen form of the bird, its curled feet, its closed eyes and smoothed feathers.

Another evening I pace the cabin, bored, and then Jorge puts on Mexican Institute of Sound to listen to while doing the dishes, and I am dancing in front of the woodstove with the baby, cradling my taut belly with one hand, and with the other doing that horrible pointing-at-the-ceiling gringa dance that prompts Jorge to ask, "Where does that come from? Why do you people do that?" but I don't care because I am making jerky little circles on one foot singing *"Katia, Tania, Paulina y la Kim."* I convince Jorge to join me on the rug, and we are both sticking out our hips, putting on satirical versions of those sexy disco faces, the logs popping in the fire and the baby a nebulous presence, rocked in my belly under the warmth of my palm.

One night in the thick gray plod of February, I stand at the sink doing the dishes with Jorge, feeling glum and jealous. He has booked a wedding in Brisbane and will spend nearly two weeks in Australia in April. I will be at thirty-one weeks when he leaves, and although the midwife said that it'd be fine for me to go with him, I decide to stay. I wash with a sad little set to my mouth, and Jorge dries and puts pots away, and I warn him not to get attacked by a kangaroo because they can be vicious.

"What do I do?" he says. "How do I avoid an attack?"

"Let's role-play it," I say. "You be the Mexican and I'll be the kangaroo."

So Jorge shuffles along with the look of a clueless *güey*, pretending to be carrying a boom box that is playing tinny *rancheritas* about unrequited love.

"*Dónde puedo comprar mis frijoles?*" he asks, hamming it up, and then I lunge at him and rake my razor-sharp kangaroo claws across his face. He shouts and drops the boom box.

"*No mames!*" he pants when he finally fends me off. "*Eres un bruto!*"

"No one sees it coming," I say. "Again."

We run through several scenarios, with the Mexican alternately eating his taco or downing a shot when a bloodthirsty marsupial charges from the ether to take him down.

Pregestation, these are scenes I cannot imagine: Would we simply not have the time for them? Would we be drinking Bell's Two Hearted and reading *New Yorkers*? Would we be too sophisticated and exposed to urban culture for live reenactments of animal attacks? Or would I simply not remember them: would they be absorbed into a larger sense of mission and purpose that clouded the everyday?

These are strange gifts that months ago I never would have labeled as gifts. Lying in bed in the morning as I lie in bed now, sometimes for forty-five minutes, sometimes an hour, which would have been unimaginable six months ago, scratching the scruff of my husband's beard and murmuring fat jokes in Spanish: *"Tu mamá es tan gorda que . . ."*

Or in the afternoon, Jorge going to the mailbox: the spring birdsong of robins, cardinals, and red-winged blackbirds strung across the hills; the crunch of gravel; the rush of brown water; the world washed, chilly and thawed. I am present to it in a way that is both incorporeal and fully embodied. I've forfeited all the forward-looking ambition of my typical awareness, and there remains an unfamiliar, essential me: here on one afternoon that will become another and another and another, each day a diaphanous screen laid over the next, their sameness transparent and simple. The sun sinks toward the prickly ridge of purple-brown trees, the dogs sit shoulder to shoulder in expectation, tails curling in opposite directions. We are all waiting for Jorge to come back and we stand watching his slow approach, envelopes in hand, beneath the heavy spring sky. This afternoon takes on the quality of a dream, of life lived outside of time.

This second trimester is the slow recognition of the fact that pregnancy is altered attention. Attention is a form of possession, a taking control of the world and shaping it in one's mind. Historically, attention has been described by philosophers and researchers as a spotlight, an isolating of certain information as relevant, interesting, and important within the overwhelming array of sensory input coming at us at all times. Attention is inseparable from expectation and meaning: our expectations, in the process of paying attention, exclude what they presume irrelevant and then fit the relevant into familiar patterns, from which we construct meaning. Then the cycle repeats itself. Attention, without expectation in particular, without knowing what to look for and why, falters; it flattens and broadens. Meaning vaporizes.

In the United States, this is generally taken as negative. Not only in the context of school, in which paying attention means processing a specific set of information in a limited time, but also in work and life, in which attention is an increasingly valuable currency. The opposite of attention is distraction, the scourge of the Internet era. U.S. notions of attention and its value haven't changed much since William James's seminal description in *The*

Principles of Psychology, volume 1: "Attention . . . is the taking possession by the mind, in clear and vivid form, of one out of what seem several simultaneously possible objects or trains of thought. It implies withdrawal from some things in order to deal effectively with others, and is a condition which has a real opposite in the confused, dazed, scatterbrained state which in French is called *distraction.*"

Maria Popova, founder of the curation site *Brain Pickings,* uses James in 2016 to illustrate the dangers of contemporary multitasking and to emphasize the value of attention in an era in which it is increasingly fractured. Yet in pregnancy I find that this war over attention has a very American flavor of dominance, reducing the world to what we can use to shape further expectation, confining it to the categories of relevant and irrelevant, of purposeful and useless, of the center and the fringe.

James wrote, "My experience is what I agree to attend to. Only those items which I notice shape my mind."

This is on one hand universal and on the other quintessentially American: notice the recurring *I* and *my. My experience, my mind.* Attention, ultimately, is the world filtered through my seeing, shaped by my expectation, my ego, my struggle for meaning. To some extent, there is no way to avoid this. There is a degree to which we must pay attention in order to function on a daily basis; without a filter for all the sensory information perpetually surging around us, we lose a sense of direction and reality, flounder in stunned passivity, sink even into mental illness. Yet there also might be value in loosing our attention from its tight leash, letting it drift without clinging to tasks, bearings, narratives. In contrast to the emphasis on attention as a spotlight beamed from the head of a discerning "I," Zen and Buddhist traditions envision the highest form of attention as dissolving the barriers between the self and the world, as paying attention not only to this rock or that thought but the whole of life now and forever, the self within it and also the self as inseparable from it.

This seems a mystical platitude until five months of pregnancy have wiped my mind clean of purpose and function, and my attention is a mist resting lightly on leaves, snow-damp bark, the perked ears of dogs, the nascent trilliums, my dad struggling to explain something about rabbits in Spanish. I am a distinct presence in this rumbling changing body, with round ligament pain occasionally doubling me over as I run, leaving me panting and wincing, awed to feel my hips wresting themselves open as I place my heavy footfalls on the snow. At the same time, the barrier between myself and the woods, the world, my family, has become permeable; without my obsessed focus on tasks, productivity, and direction, my attention eases out like a river into a delta. I do not impose myself so much as flow and sink into it all like water into sand. I sit on the front porch eating my giant bowls of crunchy yogurt, a concoction I swear to

Jorge that if we ever one day open a coffee shop we will sell for eight dollars a bowl, potent as it is with granola, Greek yogurt, chia seeds, walnuts, fruit, flax, and abundant raw honey. I give it to a friend when she comes to visit and it knocks her out for four hours. When I finish it, I sit back against one of the porch beams and rest my palm on my belly, feeling the crunchy granola arrive at the baby, her kicks and rolls. With the warmth of my new blood and insulation I can sit in the pale cold sun for a long stretch without getting a chill. I close my eyes and, without ever labeling or realizing it as such, meditate. My body takes me there more than my mind. Some days I feel like one of the posters of the human circulatory system in Mr. Wieland's ninth-grade biology classroom, all of the veins and muscles transparent, the head a goulash of swirling wires, the hands splayed open as if to say, *This is it.*

Like this, I notice woolly worms, I notice flickers on the walnut tree, I notice once the perfect carapace of a molted grasshopper. Perhaps *notice* is too active and directed a term. I see without beaming that spotlight of me, without making sense of, without organizing, without rushing what I see into language. Pregnancy for me becomes a way of unlearning, the words I know and use so confidently and thoroughly trailing behind me like the alphabet that floats through cartoons, As and Zs adrift over the budding oaks. I write in my journal, I write a few essays, but these feel less like meticulously crafted art than like natural specimens carefully pasted into a collector's notebook. Mostly I wait, my attention both suspended and everywhere, here.

Meanwhile it seems everyone else is out in the world traveling and seeing, checking in with me on the phone or Skype to report their findings. My sister goes to Boston for a conference and calls to say she's bought the baby children's books, that she went for a transcendent run on the Charles River, that she saw African American kids steal from a Muslim shop owner and yell racist taunts at him as they ran away. I respond and offer my thoughts while padding around the cabin, touching my belly whenever she asks about the baby. Jorge comes crackling through a horrible Skype connection from Sydney and announces that he witnessed a car crash via his hostel window, and also that he is heading to a koala sanctuary.

"Take a picture of a pregnant koala for me, okay?" I ask, and he promises. Ultimately I will have to settle for a pregnant kangaroo, which I accept. All of these updates, my sister seeing ponytailed Harvard grads jogging along the gray river, Jorge watching pelicans gobble up tossed fish on the Australian coast, seem to belong to another world, not only thousands of miles from me but also far away in a land where people actively notice and have experiences and accomplish tasks and stride purposefully from one day to the next. I, meanwhile, circle round and round like a hamster, from crunchy yogurt to crunchy yogurt, run to run, pasture to pasture, and yet in doing so I learn to let go of the Charles River and the Gold Coast and pregnant kangaroos and all the sorting and highlighting of the world and to be a human animal, to be smelling moss and hauling my unwieldy self up hills and reading on the porch and eating olives with my dad and not thinking about what else and why and whether or how any of it matters.

In my desk I keep the photos of the twelve- and twenty-week ultrasounds and revisit them when I begin to drown in my waiting, using them as touchstones, as reminders that this is a temporary period and not an eternity of Ritz crackers and mysterious twangs from tendons I did not know existed. In the first the baby is still a peanut, a little rounded peanut with legs, and the legs are my favorite part. The ultrasound technician took a photo just of them, chunky and so babylike it is astonishing. I show the legs to everyone as proof that there is a real baby in there, a chubby one, with little feet and everything, as I myself am still astounded by this.

The twenty-week photos are more detailed, and in one the baby's skull is visible in her now-big head, in another her heart is a black blur, and in some her arms and legs are reaching and stretching. Her butt is a butt, her belly is a belly. At this ultrasound the technician presses the wand into my belly, curves it around with a divinatory concentration, and says, "It's a girl!" My breath halts, and then I look at Jorge and say *"Una niña!"* in scratchy words half caught in my throat. In the parking lot I call each member of my family and announce, all choked up, "A girl!" This has been my intuition all along, but I haven't voiced it. Now I feel my heart clutch with new love for her, as if she has made me proud by confirming my instinct. With a name, the Elena we've had in mind from the beginning, she comes a shade closer to personhood. We call Jorge's mom on Skype from a Whole Foods in Columbus, and Jorge shouts via this crackly connection to his mountain village, *"Una niña! Qué? Una niña! Niña! Es niña!"* His mom still doesn't hear and people are staring at us as they browse the piled oranges and I am holding my belly as if it hangs in the balance and finally Jorge breaks through with an *"Es niña!"* and I hear laughter and clapping.

It occurs to me several days later that the baby, now feminine, now Elena, feels far more concrete than I do. As she has accrued substance, as she radiates from the center of me, I have become more scattered, less imposing, less of the world while also more a being of purely physical awareness. Motherhood, I grow to realize in these first months and years, is the experience of everywhere-and-nowhere-ness. It is to be the only answer to a very specific set of physical needs and it is also to be a psyche, a cosmos, an aura through which another being sees, passes, exists. The waiting of pregnancy is the liminal training period for this reality, preparing me in its timeline and timelessness, in its dissipated attention and porousness, in its tentative knowledge of the body and the heart, for the new paradigm of motherhood. Waiting sands down my acute seeing into a quieter absorption of interior shifts, and at the same time it builds my baby's fingernails one by one, her fine silk eyelashes, and one day, while I sense myself as little more than the low blue fog of morning over the pastures, she opens her eyes and gets her first glimpse of light.

Despite my increasing waddle, my widening and tautening belly, I can't believe that this gestation is moving forward and will end. I wake up thinking, *I have two months to go. I have six weeks to go.* And yet knowing where the day fits in the scheme of days counting down to June 12 makes no difference. Each day is also just one among many, and no matter how closely I follow their orbits from sunrise to sunset, how aware I am of the day before and after, their essential monotony is more apparent than their progression.

The biggest surprise of pregnancy, however, is not this relationship to time but the revelation that in the monotony lies a kind of release. Waiting has become an art, a state of suspended grace, an alternate way of living. For the first time in my life, I understand the concept of home. Home is not only a refuge, a locus of warmth and routine and familiarity, the spot where the placenta will be buried beneath the old oak tree, but a sense of peace with contradiction. It is a giving in, an acceptance, the place where I finally strip life of all its decor of aspiration and regret and let it be what it is, where it is, and nothing more. It is the space in which I forgo both anticipation and nostalgia, the space to which I let myself belong. It is a space whose defining chronological units are not days or weeks or months but the moment and the broad sweep: the first acutely felt in its passing, the other almost annihilating in its breadth.

I used to have a romantic, Polaroid-derived notion of moments. I thought of them as dramatic cinematic swellings, with me as their star. There I was on the boat deck in Borneo, and there atop a Patagonian peak, and there dancing at 4:00 a.m. on a beach by the south Indian sea. In them I was not so much myself but rather a Sarah an admiring audience would see: a character, exotic and intrepid and wild. They were crystallizations of an already perfect nostalgia.

At the same time, I longed for a secret that would be mine alone. This wild exteriority, imagining myself as a character, sometimes made me crave a sort of still pool within myself. I don't think I fully understood this longing until I was pregnant, and my interiority became all-consuming. Then I recognized—warily, with uncertainty—the secret I'd longed for, the still pond only I could visit. The secret was not just the baby inside me but my whole life, the mystery of it, its contradictions, its ultimate insignificance, its absurd particularities that only I can know and observe and appreciate.

I am reading in the armchair, bored with reading,

bored with the plod of the everyday. I ask our German shepherd to shake. I toss her ball and she plunges after it, clumsy in this tiny cluttered space. Jorge scoops it from her clenched teeth, tells her to sit and stay, positions himself on a rug opposite her. He places the ball between his feet. She is on high alert, her huge ears perked and eager. He narrates in a Televisa voice-over.

"*Se prepara la fuzzy. Se prepara el jugador. Se prepara. La fuzzy. A ver si se puede, a ver si aguanta, la fuzzy, la fuzzy, la fuzzy!*" and he shoots and the dog lunges to the left, but the ball whizzes past her outstretched paw and slams into the back door.

"*Goooooooooooooooooooooooool!*"

I laugh. The fuzzy drools. He repeats. My whole life swirls into this moment like a penny down a wishing well.

This is not the glorious encapsulation of pursued romance, observed admiringly by an imaginary audience, but rather a fleeting feeling of wholly inhabiting my life, sensing at once its scope and smallness. That is grace: not having to see from the outside and label, not seeking or glorifying or expecting, instead peeling back layers to reveal a baseline mystery where everything is connected and where nothing matters as I once thought it did.

At other times, pregnancy remains a grating tedium, a seemingly interminable haul. I slog through the pastures, the mud sucking at my muck boots, and feel an irritated dullness behind which pulses insight, unvoiced. The woods are a sloped bulletin board of pinprick trees, and my eyes can weave through that gray winter space between them on and on. It is impossible to imagine a green density filling all this in, obscuring the stark lines of trunks and pressing fleshy into the paths.

In March, at the beginning of my third trimester, my mom sends me a time-lapse video that's gone viral on YouTube. A singer took a photo of his wife every day of her pregnancy; she stands facing him in their bedroom, in the same position throughout nine months, and we watch her belly grow, her arms bulk out, her posture shift back slightly, the singer crooning to her all the while from the present on the other half of the frame. Finally, she turns, waves good-bye, and reappears with baby in arms, and she and the singer unite and embrace. It is thrilling to see time at our command like this, captured like an exotic cat in a cage. We make it perform tricks—nine months flipping by in three minutes—and we recoup our control over that long murky period of gestation.

I want, in a bout of impatience, to witness spring's blooming on camera. I suggest to Jorge that he make a time lapse of the greening, setting up a tripod in the pastures. I want this transformation to be sped up and made visible. I want to replace the slow gradual unknowing of the everyday with a clear trajectory. But my husband slacks off, and the season goes on in its incremental, gradual way. The cherry trees sprout their first buds, and one day the daffodils have opened, and then spring beauties spread like scattered white confetti around the newly green grass. Spring comes quiet and piecemeal: a ripening, a rehearsal for the full riot of summer. This is why I have always preferred fall, which is sudden and short and violent in change and color. Spring demurs constantly to winter, warming and then cooling again, sprouting bits of white and green amid mud and gray.

I sit on the rock by the creek and try to imagine the opposite slope a riot of ferns, canopied with the lanceolate leaves of shagbark hickories and the green teardrops of the beeches. Try to imagine walking up the creek in the heat, a baby in arms, sweaty tangles of vines and flowers clamoring up the banks. But my imagination, or my desire for projection forward or back, fails, and I sink again into that state of porous consciousness. Waiting, fringed with boredom. If I can push through that boredom, I sense, I can get somewhere, I can reach a different type of understanding. I fidget within it even as part of me marvels. I still want delineations, satisfactions, the stakes of past and future, the purposefulness of linearity, but all I can do is sit on that rock by the creek and wait until I see that all we're ever doing is waiting; the rest is an illusion.

One afternoon, we go for a walk in the rain. We wind up into the woods, which are softened and rendered woolly. I have in my pocket a Babybel cheese, hard and round, and I strip off its red wrapper. I have to be conscious now of eating regularly or I start to shake. As we walk I peel a boiled egg, scattering fragments of shell on the path. I eat the salty white cheese with the egg, followed up by a Ritz cracker. The trees cluster and thin. We cross the creek, we start up through the evergreen lycopodiums. What I like about hiking is this steady forward movement with no real purpose, one step after another, eating cheese, rising and descending, picking our way over logs, traversing a shelf with a view of distant ridges. All of it mimics the passing of days, and this bare, easy metaphor gives me comfort. "Days are where we live," wrote Philip Larkin. In hiking I accept this without pretentions or justifications or decoration.

Stopping to pee, squatting in the leaves, I can for the first time imagine being eighty. Can imagine my whole life blurring by to eighty, and beneath all the change and the difference this same feeling of being in the woods in the rain with the smell of wet leaves and the sky an infinite textured gray.

I am waiting for my baby, waiting for summer, waiting for knowledge, but the waiting itself becomes the knowledge and then, even as I am so hungry for transition I am practically clawing out of my skin, I begin to mourn and maybe to fear the fading of this particular consciousness: the Zen state, the acid trip of gestation, and its changed relationship to time. I wonder if I will remember that time swirls one day into the next no matter all our measurements and machinations, and that an awareness of this heightens certain moments—the giddy tittering of a boiling egg, a cool rock at the side of a creek—to the level of liberation.

At the beginning of my pregnancy and my time on the farm, I vowed to learn the names of the trees, the insects, the wildflowers, and I stacked guides a foot high on my desk. I imagined the woods as a site of mastery. In the course of a year I would walk through here like a park ranger, pointing out details to my sister with a confident expertise: the mayapples, the spicebush, the rich beds of decay that nurse morel mushrooms. But I haven't mastered anything. Not because I haven't tried, or have failed, but because I have come instead into the awareness that mastery and knowledge are perhaps two different goals: one linear, a progression, and the other circular, a repetition. In the course of this year the obsession with mastery has given way instead to an awareness of how slow, incremental, experiential, and back and forth knowledge is. How it comes in fits and starts. How in its rawest form it is incredibly hard-won and difficult to put to use. How it is kneaded like dough by the impalpable, sometimes maddeningly slow and boring roll of days, and then how it rises abruptly in one moment. How we forget the taste of that moment and have to learn again in the slow kneading. It is as much a random gift—hard cheese in the rain—as it is the intention of the seeker, the cataloging of small creatures.

Waiting at the bend in the driveway for Jorge to return with the mail, trilliums blooming now, spring peepers seeking mates with their insistent singing by the pond, one evening among many. I watch his slow return, step after step. I release the dogs and they caper around him in leaps and yips.

"Anything for us?" I ask, and he shakes his head.

The gravel drive bites into muck boots. The sky is shaded rose-violet behind us. Spring rolls into summer into fall into winter and over and over again. At some point I will get sucked back into human chronology, obsessed again with dominating it. But I hope to remember the strange delicacy of this year, hope the knowledge has penetrated deep enough that it will remain even when I can pretend I am no longer waiting. In the meantime, there is the high gurgling love song of frogs, the new thickness of the grass around my ankles.

MILDRED, MILLIE, GRANDMA MENKEDICK

THE STORY I TELL most about my grandmother is one I did not know when she was alive. It is the most dramatic and evocative of all the stories about her, and the shadow of its implications falls over her whole life and consumes her. The story begins with her husband dying a prolonged and painful death from meningitis. She was left with two sons, ages two and four. It was 1952.

When the nuns came to her door, she was facing a life of single motherhood and the scrutiny and pity of her working-class neighbors in Cincinnati. I picture the nuns as long faced, one short and one tall, all dour inevitability and efficiency.

"Mildred," they said, "we'll take your boys."

And my grandma, standing alone on that threshold, replied,

"I will never give up my sons."

I could play this story over and over like a chorus. *Ba dee da dum*, the day the nuns came to her door, *ba dee da dum*. I have its beat and rhythm down. It offers such a crisp break between past and present, such an intoxicating swell of commitment, defiance, and certainty. *This is who I am. This is where I belong.* I crave this like salt, with a stark, dry lust. It is the essence of storytelling, one moment that crystallizes and changes everything. It is the story as touchstone: I can almost reach out and stroke its smoothness.

It encapsulates the fact that my grandmother worked full-time and raised her kids as a single mother in the 1950s, and makes of this fact a decision, an identity, a fate. At her funeral we unspooled all of her life from the thread of that single story: her role as a mother and grandmother, the sacrifices it entailed, her toughness and resilience.

And yet there was also the woman I knew from the photo albums I thumbed again and again, in search of clues to who I was and where I came from: the woman who stood alone beside a purple seascape; the one laughing out of the blackness of a hotel balcony in Europe; the one who posed with an obscure sense of duty before a swath of gaping wilderness, her hair bound by a thin plastic rag. The one who went to Hawaii by herself, made friends with a fellow septuagenarian from Michigan, and hit up every bar on the coast. This was the woman who, when I asked what were the best years of her life, answered, "My sixties and seventies." The years we knew her least.

I used to go to Grandma's apartment in Cincinnati and drag all of her McAlpin's boxes of photos and itineraries and travel literature onto her kitchen table, where I'd dig through them and ply her memory for stories. She enjoyed it, but her enjoyment came less from wallowing in the past than from the immediate pleasure of spending time with her granddaughter. She paid less attention to the yellowing photos, the creased missives from the Syca-more Seniors to please bring a hat and arrive promptly at 8:00 a.m., than to the camaraderie of two people sitting together at a table on a winter afternoon.

I, however, was seeking nostalgia. I wanted to hear tales like the ones I told about South America, about get-ting to the top of a mountain, alone, and sitting in high grasses and watching the fog rise and being twenty-two and thinking of death, oh! I wanted the formation and transformation of a self.

"How was this festival, Grandma, with all the flowers?"

"It was pretty."

"What was it for?"

"Oh, it was a way to make money. You know, they call it a festival and all these tours come."

Pause. I tried again.

"You went to a belly-dance show. Do you remember that? What was it like?"

"Oh, they just dance around, move their stomach all over."

There was no prying it out of her because there was nothing to pry out; she hadn't mythologized her own experiences. She had not made of her life a story, with moments that revealed who she was and wasn't, or who she had become. Had she told me the story of the nuns, she would have recounted it with the same stolidity afforded the belly-dance show: the nuns came, she said she would not give up her boys, and she did not. But she also did not see that moment, or any moment in particular, as the catalyst for a forever-changed Mildred Menkedick. She was Mildred before, and she was Mildred after, and Mildred was above all a human being wearing white polyester slacks and beaded sweaters—one day raising children, the next riding the Ferris wheel in Saint Louis. I used to see this refusal of narrative as a limitation, a form of self-preservation or denial or ignorance; only now do I see the emancipation in it, its wisdom.

Mildred Menkedick had a helmet of snow-white hair, which she had done once a week at the beauty parlor. It was the single expense of her life that might be considered superfluous. She slept with her head suspended off the edge of her bed so as not to ding the immaculate globe of hair; her neck was stolid as an oak. I spent years trying to start an essay with that hair. But each time I'd wander into a labyrinth of anecdotes. Trying to point them toward one conclusion or self felt strained for a reason I couldn't yet grasp.

What I've come to see in the past year of pregnancy, birth, and early motherhood is the brittleness and fallibility and aspirational tidying up of stories, their weakness for redemption and their tendency to constrict and contain. Staring at the photos of Grandma here beneath a bronze statue of a general on horseback, here beside a cactus, here stern with a hand on the hood of a station wagon, here in a toga with a man also in a toga, drinking champagne, I see not stories but a life lived and improvised in an endless sequence of changes, life as a series of sparks thrown in perpetual defiance of a core self. I see not a tightly braided thread of narrative but the silky filaments of milkweed, scattered hither-dither around the pastures: the self a thousand drifting seeds, some of which grow and some of which lie dormant and some of which float on and on.

For many people, there is no transformation that rewrites their story more dramatically than parenthood, nor a single experience that begs more for narrative than their child's birth. I am no different. But for me sometime late in pregnancy, an awareness of the limitation of story, of its ultimate inability to capture the perpetually changing self, becomes as vivid as the need to shape and tell my own story. Now these two desires—to acknowledge all that stories reduce, hem in, and minimize, and also to honor my story as the meaning at the core of my own life—vie constantly for control. What I've come to wonder is at what point our stories are mirages that mask the ephemeral, immediate realities of our lives, reducing their complexities to a single dimension, and at what point stories have the capacity to anchor us, encourage us to pay closer attention to our changing selves, and to become more compassionate, open, and whole versions of those selves.

I spend the first half of my pregnancy flailing in a new and frightening uncertainty, grieving the imagined loss of my self as defined by a list of countries and experiences. The story I've been telling over and over again for the past decade reveals itself as just that: a story. One that, once I stop telling it, will no longer define me. Then who will I be?

So I build a narrative of transformation: the liminal period of gestation will remake me and I will emerge a mother above all. I will become a better person, my harder, selfish edges tamed by a year of walking in snowy woods with a growing and enlivening belly, a mind slowed and deepened. This is the story I still tell myself and still believe, the clearly marked channel I shovel all of my uncertainties and imaginings into, but in the second half of pregnancy I come to understand it as a story. That is, even after the breakthroughs, the moments standing in the half-frozen creek praying to a gray sky, the afternoons of weeping, the hours of writing in journals with a cup of lemon tea to fend off nausea, even after the rewriting of my story, I am repossessed by doubt or longing or simple fear. I come to see that I can never eliminate them, that perhaps never again will my story seem so straightforward or my identity so clear as a rung bell.

Sometime in late winter, on one of many long gray drives back to the farm from Columbus, my husband and I get in a fight about a girl he loved when he was growing up. She was not a girlfriend, but one of those first loves that imprint on us forever, on our very understanding of love. I want reassurance that he does not love this girl any longer. In the ambiguity of the afternoon and twenty weeks of pregnancy, with my future foggier than ever, I want this certainty. "You have no more feelings for her," I say. Normally, he would agree. *Yes, no feelings.* But perhaps the destabilizing rawness of pregnancy has robbed him of the ability to tell such a simple and conclusive story. He shrugs. He says, "Well, of course there are still feelings, but not love," and I flip out. "What kind of feelings? What do you mean 'not love'?" As any member of any long-term relationship will recognize, it is the beginning of a rapid and dramatic descent into hairsplitting arguments about the terminology of affection. He fights back asking if my similarly charged relationship with an ex-boyfriend is over, if I no longer have any feelings for him. And so we spend the afternoon inflaming old sensitivities to pointless soreness, struggling for a clarity neither of us will achieve and yet also, in this tentative space of gestation, fighting toward a nascent understanding of ambiguity.

When we return it is evening, and that dramatic mazarine curtain of winter dusk in the Midwest has fallen. We are walking up a snowy abandoned road. The night is silken with cold and blue. The shadows of branches crisscross us, our interlinked arms. I feel a new adult understanding of messiness, an acceptance of the constant overlapping of past with present, love with love, self with self. I understand that they will forever blur into one another, circle back around one another, retain disordered contradictions like tidal pools arranged and rearranged with each wave. For a moment, I make peace with this understanding. We traipse across the furrowed snow of the yard, stand for a minute beneath the full moon, crawl together under the quilts in the bedroom. On that evening I grasp that perhaps this is all we can do: recognize the ways we struggle to sand our rough lives into tangible and comprehensible stories, and acknowledge the desires and fears that drive that refining process.

Still, I continue rewriting my own story. My dedication to literature grows in direct proportion to my awareness of its limitations, its inventions. In the same way that the straightforward march of the pregnancy timeline makes time less acute, less real, the awareness that stories cannot and will not adhere to lived life makes me more determined to write.

I embrace the wholesale reappropriation of self that comes with pregnancy, and at the same time I circle back to question it, I juggle both its ultimate uncertainty and the need for it as an anchor. I rewrite myself in clouds and mornings, luna moths and rain, in repetition more than plot, and I rewrite myself in habits, in the regular phone calls to my mom, the slow walks, the new books and ways I read, the generosity and intimacy placed on the pedestal once reserved for intrepidness. There are times when I merge with motherhood—to borrow an image of Annie Dillard's I've always loved—like a body diving into its reflection in a pool. Walking up the driveway one chilly spring afternoon I feel my belly beneath an old gray sweater, feel my gentle walk, my husband's gaze, and I am a mother. It is a brief alignment, one of those tidy few we're given in which we can see ourselves clearly in new roles, in which the murkiness, the back and forth, the uncertainty of our lives, cohere to match the stories we tell.

Daily life can rarely compete with story; we tell ourselves over and over that one day we will arrive at a certain point, we will have become a certain type of person living in a certain type of place with a certain type of lifestyle, but once we're there we're still scratching the dog behind the ears and examining our split ends in the mirror, waking up every day to shuffle around the kitchen while the espresso rumbles up its fount. Daily life overwhelms the gleaming vision of story with all of its familiarity, ordinariness, detail. We dwell perpetually in the story of our expectations and only rarely notice how they've merged with the quotidian, how they actually manifest themselves, before we have constructed and are chasing another set.

At the end of Richard Linklater's film *Boyhood,* Patricia Arquette sits amid boxes of her son's belongings in his college dorm room, where, after eighteen years of child-rearing, she will finally leave him to fend for himself. In the course of the film she's gone from a stressed-out, broke single mother, shuttling her kids around in a cramped car with the windows down, running from ruinous marriage to ruinous marriage, to a self-possessed professor with two kids in college and a comfortable middle-class house. She begins to cry, and her son asks what's wrong. "I just thought there'd be more," she says. In her comment is the whole of parenthood, the whole sweep of a life, and it is not sad or bitter: it just *is,* an inevitable part of our nature.

On a hike in late May, when the woods are beginning to exude that tropical breath of midwestern summer, it occurs to me that I'm actually doing what I've always said to Jorge that we should do: live without worrying about productivity, take advantage of our impoverished artisthood by being present in the everyday: cooking and hiking and thinking and reading and not subscribing to formulas. And it's enlightening, it's great, I recognize the incredible luck of being able to appreciate it, but it remains everyday life—there isn't the perpetual wash of amazement or satisfaction one imagines, or it comes in unexpected moments. We are still all wrapped up in the tumble of days, the basic gestures of maintaining our lives.

I begin to have frequent Braxton-Hicks contractions, during which my belly is a fist clenching tighter and tighter around the baby and my organs. I have the sensation at each contraction's peak that all of my bodily energy is coursing into the rock of my middle and hardening there. Gradually, my belly loosens until again it blends seamlessly—as seamlessly as it can when it sits like a soccer ball on my hips—with the rest of me.

We have the first bonfire of the season, that primal smear of flame licking toward the huge obsidian sky. The lightening bugs are out now, a million zigzagging shimmers over the pastures, in the woods like glitter tangled in dark hair. The sky is so thick with stars the constellations seem to jumble together. Dad, Meg, visiting family, Jorge, and I sit in chairs drawn close to the pit. Jorge steps back to take a photo, and it occurs to me that this is the first bonfire we've had since the one just before I found out I was pregnant. I could not imagine what it would be like to be pregnant, then what it would be like to be four, seven, nine months pregnant. I cannot imagine now what it will be like to give birth, to have a newborn, and then a child. These are the first experiences of my life I have been unable to imagine at all. Of course I have visions drawn from friends and media, but they go no further than me, say, nursing in a rocking chair or hiking with the baby through the woods. I have no sense of what the day-to-day substance of the experience will consist of, and this highlights for me the absurdity of expectation.

By the time I am pregnant, queasily taking teensy bites of blueberry bagel and reading Erdrich, by the time I am at the twenty-week scan saying *"Una niña!,"* by the time the Braxton-Hicks confirm that labor is real and imminent, each of these states has become—while exciting, while emotional—normal and assimilated. They've descended from the realm of story to the everyday. Even this bonfire, which I use as a marker to signify the near closing of this period of gestation, is one of many bonfires. They are significant because I assign to them this human, symbolic weight, this vision and description, but now I can also say, *Here I am again at the bonfire, my huge belly reaching toward the heat, my hand resting atop it to feel the occasional explorations of a small foot; here I am with no beer, not even a desire for one, and this is now.* The farm accentuates this: here again the fireflies, tricking out maple lane in gold dazzle; here again the first high chime of the crickets; here again the fire, the faces, older and lined, hair thinned, glasses or not, staring with the same primitive daze into the flame, and here the stories, the children, the years.

Stories have themes and characters. I wanted to make of my grandma a character, but I realized that I had not one but many characters: the Millie who gamely wore the same outfit for a week in Spain after the tour bus ran over her suitcase, and the Mildred who forced a medieval torture device of a hairbrush through my tomboy hair before dinner; the Millie who never spoke of her husband and never dated or remarried, and the woman who fell asleep listening to the truckers on shortwave radio. The grandma who asked my dad "When is she going to get a job?" after I'd been living hand to mouth overseas for years, and the grandma who, when I confessed in her living room at the Seasons that I didn't know what to do with my life, responded, "Well, that's okay," and meant it. The one who said when I moved to China, "Well, at least it's not Mexico," and the one whose diminutive white-haired friend approached me in the Seasons dining room and said, "So you're the granddaughter from Mexico! We've heard so much about you."

It could be argued that these are simply different sides of the same woman, manifestations of the multifaceted-ness of any character, but I believe they are also different women, selves that didn't fit into other selves with the tidy alignment of *matryoshka* dolls. This I couldn't under-stand until I became a mother. I so completely inhabited my own story that I failed to see its construction, its ulti-mate flimsiness—the way I had cut myself out of it like a chain of paper dolls, so many one-dimensional selves holding hands into infinity.

Story gets addictive. A little quickly snowballs into a lot, especially in times of uncertainty. In the final stretch of my pregnancy, after seven months of living in a cabin on a remote plot of land in southeastern Ohio with little for narrative other than the changing days and seasons, with the tremendous and indefinite event of birth on the horizon, I grasp at whatever story I can. A robin builds its nest in a nook between two beams on the back porch. We see it gathering dried grasses, sticks, bits of hay, twisting them into habitable form with a pragmatism that reminds me of the women selling fruit on the streets of Mexico, shearing papaya neatly of their skins. Sometime after the nest has been established, Jorge and I peek in to discover four pale blue eggs, and from then on I glance outside every so often to check for scrawny hatchling necks poking above the rim. One morning in doing so I see only absence in the nook where the nest has been: a view clear through to the woods. I look down. There, on a bed of rocks, is the overturned nest. Beside it are two baby birds, tiny, splayed, and wet looking.

Hugely pregnant, my heart a lump in my throat, I rush outside to investigate and then kneel down beside the babies. The thin reptilian skin of their chests is transparent, exposing the red and blue tangles of their insides. Their bodies rise and fall infinitesimally, each breath a minuscule palpitation in a world that suddenly seems enormous and loud, full of crashing branches and prowling dogs.

I pick up a stick, hold my breath, and poke each of them. Their beaks snap open instantly, like toys. One is more vigorous than the other. Looking closer I see that there are tiny gray spiders crawling all over the weaker one's body. I reach down and pinch the spiders one by one, chucking them aside, strangely furious. Then I take control in the way we do in 2014: I hurry back into the cabin and Google "baby birds fell from nest." The advice of the Google hive mind is to put the birds back in and leave them alone: no one can do the job of a mama bird like a mama bird.

Feeling the enormous pressure of story, terrified of the symbolism of having baby birds die on my back porch two months before I give birth, I go outside again and wedge the nest firmly into its nook. Then I lift the birds inside one by one. Their bodies are cold and rubbery. There seems to be no elegant way of arranging them, and they wind up heaped atop one another, little beaks grasping. Finally I leave them and go back to work. But their frailty, the enormous symbolic import of their life or death, weighs on the edges of the morning and then collapses it into singular worry. I give up on work and kneel on the couch by the window, watching the nest, biting my nails, waiting for the robin mom to come back. She doesn't. For hours, with that unique capacity for thoughtless waiting that pregnancy engenders, I keep my eyes on the nest. Still she does not return. I give up and collapse on the bed upstairs, a crying blubbery mess. Eventually I come back down, make myself coffee, shuffle back over to the window. There she is, hunkered down on the nest, her simple features plain and alert.

"She came back!" I shout to Jorge.

"*Órale,*" Jorge says, nonchalant, glancing out the window before popping a cookie in his mouth and starting his own coffee. He takes the birds in stride as one more element of the morning—rain or sun, chill or warm breeze—while I teeter on a narrative knife-edge.

I spend the whole day, and the better part of the next two weeks, watching the robins. Their drama becomes my drama, their story a parallel of my own, an allegory for the perilousness and hope of birth. Eventually, I realize that the two straggly puppet strings of the babies' necks have dwindled to one; that one neck grows stronger and steadier and more self-possessed.

"What happened to the other one?" I ask Jorge, but we are too scared of frightening away the mama bird to approach the nest and look in. I watch as the mama plucks huge white poop sacs from the baby's behind and flies off to deposit them in the woods. I watch as the baby wrestles open its threadbare wings and begins to flutter them in the nest in practice flight.

On Mother's Day, there is a spring storm. I take the dogs for a walk, and when I return, invigorated at the sight of spring beauties and the blooming trilliums on the creek banks, I glance from a safe distance to see, once more, a blank space where the nest has been.

"Fucking robin mom!" I shout to Jorge. It is my first experience with that potent, primordial mix of possessiveness, blame, and guilt that characterize parenting.

The nest is overturned; beneath it I find the remaining baby. It is much bigger, stronger, healthier, opening and closing its clementine beak with vigor. The rubbery skin has sprouted the long pins that will become feathers. The pins are livid and gray-black, the colors of steel and railroad and charcoal around this tiny thundering heart. I am struck by the mixture of hard and soft, fragile and strong, witnessing the naked mechanical structures that will support the delicate grace of flight. I look at the pink clawed feet and remember the nurse at the eleven-week ultrasound: "Everything's there," she told me, showing me the legs, the feet, the tiny hand reaching up. "He or she just needs to grow." When I put the chick back in the nest it pokes up its little head, which is scruffy like a stuffed animal worn bare from so much handling, and gives a silent cry for food.

I spend the afternoon waiting for the robin to return. As the hours go by, the chick's head surges straight up: a direct, vertical plea. I get angrier. Has she given up?

Around four I go hunting for worms, scraping heavy-hearted in the bright mud by the old township road. No worms, or none my untrained eye can see. I trudge back, come inside, and see the robin perched on the edge of the nest, her big gray eye taking in our window. I feel a swelling of both love and consternation for her, want to applaud at this dramatic turn in the baby's narrative. Over the next week I watch him grow tufts on either side of his head so he looks like a little old man; see his wings fill out until their fluffiness obscures their mechanical origins entirely; catch his first endeavors to free himself from the mama robin as she clamps her haunches over him. Occasionally he succeeds in popping out from under her, and he glances around for a few seconds in dumb wonder before her warm flank wrestles him back down. She has the Hula-Hooper's ability to separate her lower body from her upper, wiggling those paunchy hindquarters while keeping her head still and poised. She becomes for me a character, a mixture of hard practicality and tender concern, somewhat like those tough and weary old market women in Mexico, somewhat like my grandma.

As my due date approaches, so does the fledgling's departure. By late May, he is nearly too big for the nest. He flaps his wings with enthusiasm, rising each time a little farther so I think, *This is it, this is it!* I want the ultimate conclusion and symbolic release of flight. But then he snuggles back into the dried grasses, until one Sunday I return from a weekend of birthing classes to realize he is gone.

For about two hours, I revel in the bittersweetness of his departure and the relief of his ultimate triumph (setting aside the Google-derived knowledge that he still has weeks of training in the wild before his survival is anywhere near certain). It is the oldest story of all time—birth, coming of age, departure—and I have witnessed it for a reason. And then I look out and see the robin tucking dried grasses into the nest. She wiggles her wide belly down, making room. *No*, I think. *No.*

"Jorge!" I shout. "She's making another freaking nest!"

At first I want him to take it down, to put up some sort of obstacle to future nest construction and symbolic peril. But in the end I don't have the heart for it. Removing the nest is such a clear editorial act that it makes me feel weak. In the end what I have witnessed is one small, raw, riveting spectacle of birth and death among many. I can craft whatever larger parable I want from it, but at the end of the day the story is my invention, and trying to get it to predict or reflect the trajectory of my life is like trying to stick a Post-it to a river.

So I watch over the last several weeks of my pregnancy as three new eggs hatch; three chicks grow and sprout feathers; three ragged necks bob and beg; three fledglings jostle one another in the too-small nest and flap their wings over one another's heads; and one morning, the nest, brimming just the day before, is empty.

My grandma died at 2:25 p.m. on March 3, 2012. My uncle Bill, my dad, and I were in the room. Grandma had entered the hospital nearly a week earlier with congestive heart failure, and the cardiologist had given her only a few days to live. Everyone was worried it was going to get much more painful: suffering, disorientation, a sharp decline. Grandma was sleeping. Dad had dozed off. Bill was working on his computer. I was reading. I was the one who looked up, for no reason, really, just looked up. I saw a stillness in her face, the only difference from a minute ago. I tapped my dad on the foot. He startled awake, and I nodded toward Grandma.

It was quiet. When the nurse came, she was astounded.

"This almost never happens," she said. She couldn't believe it. Normally, there are signs. Labored breathing, confusion, anxiety. The nurses warn people and prepare them. The nurse was silent for a moment. "Your grandmother was a strong woman," she told me. "She chose when to go."

I am almost never home. I am always the one who is not there. For holidays, births, funerals, graduations. I am always the one on a bus in South America, lost in Borneo, in a Mexican market. That semester I had taken off again for the villages of Oaxaca's Sierra Norte, missed Christmas even when I said I'd be there. But I was home for this.

I hold tight to this story as an example of a preordained connection between me and my grandma. It is the crucible for my first understanding of that space of birth and death, where everything I have taken for granted is turned on its head, and my everyday priorities, obsessions, desires, are revealed as so many baubles. I became an adult for my family on the night I stayed alone with Grandma in hospice, when I fed her a chocolate milk shake at 3:00 a.m. I had long been the baby, but then I was old enough to stay.

Yet in the years after her death, I began to see that my connection with Grandma may have been as much about what I didn't know of her life—what I couldn't know—as it was about what she and I shared. More and more when I think of that afternoon in hospice, waiting for what came next after she'd taken her last breath, I think of Marge.

Marge was Grandma's best friend for nearly seventy years. They met shortly after Earl Menkedick died, when Grandma, who as a young widow had taught herself to drive, offered Marge a ride to church. This turned into a Sunday ritual in which the two stole as much conversation as they could in the car before the kids began to whine that they were hungry. Eventually, Grandma and Marge planned a vacation together to an Ohio state park. They piled Grandma's two boys and Marge's three girls in the backseat, shared bunk beds in a cabin, and walked to the pool to take showers. They returned every summer until their kids were grown.

In 1971, Marge's husband died suddenly of a heart attack, and in 1973, when Marge's last daughter had gotten married and Grandma had been a widow for twenty-one years, Grandma and Marge took their first trip together. They went to Mexico on Cartan's Deluxe Toltec Vacation, which promised "cobblestone streets," "living history," "the most interesting exhibits on Mexico's earliest inhabitants," and "a delightful stay in Paradise."

On their first night in Mexico City, their roommate died. "You know, that sorta colored the trip," Marge explained to me at a Bob Evans in Cincinnati. Marge is Grandma's opposite in almost every way: barely topping ninety pounds, soft-spoken, dulcet of voice and manner, where my grandma was sturdy, frank, unabashed. In pictures the two look as if they've been chosen by casting directors to be paired on a marooned ship for comic effect. "Also," Marge added of this Mexico adventure, "they didn't have much electricity. It was a little bit scary." The specter of Cartan's Deluxe Toltec Vacation did not deter them: they went on to Ireland, Germany, Switzerland, the souks of Tangiers, where they were told, along with the other Sycamore Seniors, to walk in a straight line and not touch anything and not talk to anyone and to clutch their handbags firmly to their sides. They went to the world's fair in Knoxville with Grandma's boss and exhausted him and his wife in their insistence on seeing every single exhibit.

We all knew about Marge, of course. But I don't think any of us knew what Marge meant until Grandma's death.

The first time I saw Grandma cry was the day before she died, when Marge entered her room at hospice. Marge began to weep, in the same soft and sweet and steady way she speaks. Her whole body shook. Later, for a week after Grandma died, she lost feeling in her legs, and the doctors couldn't find anything wrong.

Marge held Grandma's hand, and Grandma said, in her voice grown long and low and weak from her dying heart, "I ain't gonna get any better. I'm gonna go to sleep now."

"You sleep peacefully," Marge said, patting her veined hand.

And Grandma started to cry. "We had so many good times together, I just wanted to say good-bye."

Marge was crying the kind of tears that come unconsciously, rising from some deep interior well.

"Don't say good-bye, say 'Let's meet again soon,'" Marge said.

"Keep up with the crowd," Grandma urged, and her voice was so parched, so low. In her final days, we gave her ice, over and over, to wet her lips. "Have fun. You keep having a good time without me. We've had a lot of good times together."

"I will," Marge promised.

"Good-bye, Marge," Grandma said.

"Good-bye, Millie," Marge said. She was crying so hard all she could do was wave at us through the tears, and she hurried out down the hall.

For a few minutes after she left, Grandma couldn't stop crying. The tears were like the blinding swirls of a blizzard, unstoppable, and we were helpless before them. We, my dad and I, cried too. We did not know what to say, what to do, but I think she was too gripped by this good-bye to notice us. She did not cry like this for anyone. I had never seen her so moved. Between her and Marge was another life, another story, or simply the truth that the story is never big enough to contain all of us.

· · ·

Stories organize competing desires into cause and effect and offer the reprieve of predictability and inexorability when events have unsettled our understanding of who we are. We use stories to steer ourselves in a certain direction, to create a clear wake whose dissipating V propels us. We can tell stories to lie to ourselves or to demand more from ourselves. As I come to understand that my story of transitioning from traveler to mother, from a character always looking for the faraway and the exotic to one paying close attention to the interior and the domestic, is in fact a creation, separate from and layered atop the volatile everyday, I am at first disappointed. I go through a stretch of disenchantment: it will not be so easy to structure my life or define my role, to say that my baby will always trump my writing and that I will always put the domestic before my career, to decide to purchase a small piece of earth instead of striking out on a bumpy road in some hot forsaken land. These decisions will in fact be in perpetual negotiation and, even once settled, deeds signed or suitcases packed, will never be complete, never free from uncertainty, doubt, regret, all the shoulds and should-haves and what-ifs. All I'll have is the story, which I can turn to in the moments that feel right as affirmation and call up in the moments that feel forced or rough or sad as a vow. Czeslaw Milosz wrote: "The purpose of poetry is to remind us / how difficult it is to remain just one person."

I come to see story not as flesh and blood but as religion: always invented, always subject to interpretation, and best tempered by forgiveness and doubt. At certain graceful and eternal moments, I will merge with my story, become it. I will be then a character, a photograph, a memory eulogized and recalled and passed down. But in my life I will be a girl binge-watching *The Good Wife* with a family-size box of Cheez-Its, reading poetry on the cabin porch, constantly vowing to drink less coffee, singing Celia Cruz's "La Vida Es un Carnaval" to the bashful Little Dude.

In the last week of May, I am on the cusp of giving birth. I enter a period often called nesting, referring to the powerful instinct many women have in the days before labor to organize and clean: stacking cans, scrubbing floors, getting into nooks and crannies they haven't cared about in years.

Much to Jorge's chagrin, my nesting does not take this form. I am sitting on the front porch of the cabin thinking about story. I am watching clouds, considering how the lesson of pregnancy has been not the power of story but the uncertainty of the everyday. Every single day, a new scene played out over the pastures; 270-some days of ever-changing clouds. Sometimes I feel like a mother, and sometimes I feel like a selfish wannabe bohemian full of doubt, and sometimes like a generous loving wife, and sometimes like a stifled traveler, and sometimes like a daughter come home to the farm, and sometimes all, and I come to understand that it will perhaps not get any

easier than this: that there will be no more certainty than
the rare moment of grace when we embody a certain self
completely, leaving no shadow.

My grandma kept boxes and boxes of travel relics: free
postcards from cheap hotels in Florida; yellowed photos
of ladies in practical one-pieces on Hawaiian beaches;
flattened plastic bags with the names of stores long out of
business; tiny viewfinders offering frozen and miniatur-
ized versions of herself at one or another American tour-
ist trap. One representative box, of the white variety that
had long ago contained a Christmas sweater, was labeled
PHOTOS: CLEAN OUT SOME TIME.

But she never did. She saved it all. Perhaps it was the
same Depression-era impulse that led her to hoard the
miniature bags of chips she won at senior bingo in her
dishwasher. But perhaps it was more than that. She rarely
spoke about her deceased husband, Earl, about his life or
death or their courtship. Although she never remarried,
she gave no indication of mourning or missing him. And
yet when my family and I spent an evening at her apartment after her death, going through her things, we found
a box with a birthday card that Earl had sent her when
they were dating. On the front was a duck with oversize features and a big quacky grin; inside it read "You're
my girl." "I never knew she had this," marveled my dad,
though he'd spent eighteen years living in her house.

We found boxes of thimbles. Boxes of rosaries. Boxes of tiny notepads she got for free at the bank. Boxes of key chains: some of crucified Jesus, some of hula-skirted and bikinied dancers. Boxes of handkerchiefs. Boxes of playing cards. Boxes of matches. Boxes of clipped recipes for coleslaw. Boxes of boxes of Kleenex.

"Grandma was the least nostalgic person I knew," my stepmom, Meg, told me. "She did not have a drop of nostalgia in her. She lived in the present, and that was it." Meg made a chopping motion with her hand, as if the past were a hunk of hard cheese she'd just sliced off.

And yet Grandma kept all those yellowing photos of her and Marge, all those memories from the best years of her life, disobeying her own Post-it urgings to throw them out.

And yet under the sink in the bathroom, in a shoebox, she kept tiny bottles of liquor covered in dust. I lifted one out and dangled it like a pendulum in front of my dad. He laughed, shook his head. The sample size of Bacardi rum must have been twenty years old, from a cruise or a trip to Florida. There was one sip missing. When she took it, who she was then, on a boat or a beach, chatting with Marge over roast beef in Omaha or alone in the thick of Cincinnati winter, we'll never know.

OPEN

I N MY TWENTY-NINTH WEEK of pregnancy, I am sprayed by a skunk. I am running with my dogs through the spring woods, and the mutt hound Little Dude gets on a scent. "Little Dude!" I bellow without stopping, hoping she'll fall back in behind me. I steal quick glances into the thickets where she's bolted, and my eye catches on something black, and white.

Then the scent hits. It envelops us wholly as a ski mask. Little Dude is gagging, foaming at the mouth, vomiting a thin drizzle of green. Stella, the German shepherd, paws at her muzzle and rubs herself hard against wet leaves, her eyes squeezed shut and streaming tears.

I am in shock. I shout to the dogs, *Ven, ven, ven,* kicking at the ground around their bodies. I run as fast as I can with my third-trimester belly down the old township road to the cabin, the dogs trailing me half blind. I fumble inside and call Jorge, who is on a fishing trip with my dad. The two men swing by Dandy Don's for jugs of tomato juice, which supposedly removes the scent (an old wives' tale, we discover belatedly, when the dogs reek of both rancid juice and skunk funk). By the time Dad and Jorge return, the dogs have succumbed to their punishment and are cowed, shell-shocked. The men begin the task of hosing them down, adding the insult of near-freezing water to the lingering injury of their reek. Leroy, the kingly housecat, watches with relish. He walks idly back and forth in front of the dog run, purring.

Over the next week the cabin becomes suffocating with stench until, stir-crazy and skunk numbed, we are finally driven to play Monopoly. I get so wild that I crack an O'Douls. The .05 percent alcohol and the revived childhood thrill of Monopoly hit me hard: for the first time in seven months, I feel like myself. It comes over me in a slow wave, like a drug beginning to take effect, except the drug is my old self. Jorge moves his little metal dog, and I shout, "Those are the *Chance, güey,* haven't you figured that out by now, the Community Chest are *yellow,*" and I sense my self like a ghost who has just slipped into my body.

I am surprised to discover that I no longer know what to do with my self. I do not know whether to grieve or to celebrate and so do neither: instead, I watch, which is all I have learned to do throughout my pregnancy. I watch this Sarah I have taken for granted throughout my twenties and into my early thirties, the person I thought I was, who disappeared two weeks into gestation. She is adamant and lively, she drinks, she jokes, she imposes herself on a situation, gets way out in front of it, unlike this other being who does not fill up a room so much as take it in. They are not two separate people, two separate selves. Rather, one is a self and one is not. The latter is something else: an emptiness, an openness I had not experienced before pregnancy.

Jorge wins at Monopoly as he wins at every American game: with infuriating guilelessness, despite having grown up in Mexico and never playing any of them before. I berate him for his smug little grin and his ongoing confusion of Chance and Community Chest and then lie in bed for a while feeling this old self still present, haunting. Where has she gone, and will she ever inhabit me so completely? In motherhood, will any self ever be so total, will I ever be *me* in that fully absorbed and unthinking way again? I don't know, but my intuition is no; I will never get that self back in her entirety. But what compels me is that I have lost not just my self but the notion of a self, a definable and characterizable entity separate from the world and in a binary relationship with it, variable in tastes and appearances but consistent and singular in essence.

Of course it's easy to chalk all this up to hormones, and this I did during my first trimester. I was astounded at the astronomic physical and perceptual shifts of pregnancy. I'd spent my late twenties saying cavalier things like "Oh, I'd love being pregnant, I just don't know about what comes afterward!" I thought of pregnancy like a marathon: an exotic, temporary experience of thrilling at the limits and capabilities of the body, only with a baby at the end instead of mealy sliced bagels. And then I found myself curled up in the fetal position, sobbing "Why don't they tell you it'll be like this?"

Now I realize "they"—this nebulous "they" often referenced in talk of pregnancy, referring to all the women who have come before and who were supposed to have conveyed via some sort of gender ESP the overwhelming complexity of the experience—haven't told because the most important phenomena to relate, the most significant changes, are also the most enigmatic, global, and personal. Above all, they defy the familiar language of story, with its neat transitions, its clear befores and afters. As such they are most easily defined by what they are not: *I am no longer myself.* Only when the old self shows up does the change gain outlines.

A friend of mine who miscarried at six weeks wrote me that she knew something had happened when she woke up feeling like herself again. She wasn't able to explain how she hadn't been herself, who or what she had become, only the return to the old self with its clear parameters and bearing on the world. I got the sense that her return was wrenching not only because of the loss of her baby, but also because of the loss of a brief experience of the expansiveness of pregnancy, a glimpse of annihilation both terrifying and liberating. Afterward, the self's confines seem limiting, like returning to the same dull linoleum kitchen after an afternoon in the blasting sun of a wilderness.

And yet I'd lived in that kitchen for thirty-one years and grown accustomed to its peeling countertops, its magnets and coffee stains. I miss it desperately, feverishly, angrily during the first trimester, and with a numb distance throughout the second. My previous life takes on a nostalgic dreaminess, shrouded in pearly ethereal light, like Nabokov's imperial Russia viewed from the wastes of Connecticut. It pulses from the opposite shore of pregnancy with the glow of irrevocable separation. By the third trimester, when the old me shows up for Monopoly, she has become a curiosity. The no-longer-me of pregnancy—a being who exists almost exclusively as a heavy-moving body, graced occasionally by a faint whiff of mind—has begun to guess at what so many mothers before me must have already discerned: that Sarah was a fiction, which has collapsed and left only the rubble of titles and habits.

I remember an activity in the third grade in which we were told to fill in an outline of a puppy with words that defined us. I wrote *Tacos. Babysitters Club. Fiery. Purple.* Then we laminated our newly defined selves in their dog shells. I still have that puppy in a box somewhere; it's a cute artifact of childhood, and yet my adult conceptions and presentations of self aren't much more sophisticated. I think back to all the times I've said "I am" with such vigor and certainty: I am a traveler, a writer, passionate, angry, loyal. Now more than ever, when people are summarized by profiles, we metonymize ourselves in pithy phrases: *beer drinker, lover of marshmallows*. These come to stand in for the mercurial energies that drive, confuse, frustrate, and refuse crystallization. They are the Greek ruins around which our lives swirl, ever contradictory and indefinite.

Harvard psychologist Daniel Gilbert alludes to this perpetual changeability in his discussion of the psychology of the future self. He writes: "We treat our future selves as though they were our children, spending most of the hours of most of our days constructing tomorrows that we hope will make them happy. . . . [But] our temporal progeny are often thankless. We toil and sweat to give them just what we think they will like, and they quit their jobs, grow their hair, move to or from San Francisco, and wonder how we could ever have been stupid enough to think they'd like *that*."

We disappoint our future selves because we assume they'll adhere to the same patterns, nurse the same desires, rely on the same cluster of definitions and loyalties. Implicit in this assumption is the notion of a self that is a definitive part, if not the definitive part, of existence. This self wants Twinkies, and that one wants a non-

GMO vegan nut bar, but each is clearly *a self* in relationship to the world. There is no room for a not-self in the way we think, or even in the way Gilbert writes, but in pregnancy the self is vaporized, and there is nothing to replace it.

I am blurred with the sound of crickets, blurred with my body, made part of what Suzuki calls the "great self": all mothers, all children, the natural world, the trucks that rise in a distant grind over the hill and zoom along the straightaway, the slow blue curl of evening into morning.

I find I need more time to pull away from the everyday, from email and productivity and the drive for success. I need moments in the woods, in my journal, of a deeper consciousness, or else I start to feel a rust of stress build up; I start to clang for the first time in my life against the tin walls of my ego. I take the dogs and climb the hill into the snowy woods. I take the dogs and roam the blooming pastures. I take the dogs and descend through the smell of dogwoods sweet and thick as honey.

The more of this time I take, the more of myself I scrub off of the world around me until I start to see. I go nowhere, and yet in going nowhere I am in a way I cannot be when I impose myself on the world. As the winter tips into spring and spring brightens into early summer, the world comes into relief: immediate, overwhelming, and unmediated. Instead of me there is the morning porch, the coreopsis making their slow revolution with the sun, the driveway under a starry cosmos of maples, a dog with a fly on her nose, June's orange-cream evenings fizzling into night. The bare bones of life, unadorned with expectation or seeking, only ever right now.

In week thirty-six, my colostrum comes in. I am standing at the bathroom mirror and see droplets around my left breast through my threadbare gray tee. I gawk at myself in the mirror, lean closer to inspect the liquid. It is sweet and the yellow of buttermilk. I shout for Jorge, and he stares at it with mild fear. Later that afternoon I am sitting on the porch and it starts to rain. Jorge comes running barefoot into the yard, pulls off his shirt, dances around jokingly, hopping from foot to foot, so I too strip down to my underwear and run out, raising my hands to the sky of jigsaw blue and gray, the rain a cool prickling on my skin. I look down anew at my breasts, like acquaintances long ignored, now full of intrigue and power. I squeeze them to see the new, silky droplets pour over the nipple and mix with rain.

We take the dogs for a walk when the afternoon is thick with moisture and anticipation. The light and heat change quickly: balmy blue now, shifting to slate gray and chill, and then, quick as a flicked switch, white pummeling sheets of rain. We walk through them in the pastures, laughing, drenched, squinting through the streams rolling down our faces. As we enter the woods, the storm picks up. The creek gushes and slaloms up its banks and the trees are whipped into a white froth. The ground has disappeared in a brown churn, and even the dogs have slunk down, cowering, so Jorge shouts, "Let's go back!" We turn, hurrying along the path in half thrall, half fear, and by the time we reach the pastures it's over. There is sun, friendly blue. We're soaked and dripping, our shoes squishy. We wring ourselves out and start back through the steaming thigh-high grasses. I open my dress, let my belly out, walk with my big taut body through the damp. We come over the hill of the front pasture to the view of farm and valley, my body before me, leading me slow down into the fields.

"You look like a flasher," Jorge says. "The milk mo-lester." We put the dogs in the run, check the garden for strawberries, look down the throats of the irises at their striped tongues.

"Enlightenment," Suzuki writes, "is like hearing a bugle or smelling tobacco for the first time."

We strip off our dripping clothes, shower, tumble into bed. The afternoon softens and I lay before the fan, Jorge curled behind me, smelling of soap.

Every day in the barn, my brother plays the same notes on the saxophone. Jack is using the farm as a way station between New York City—where he worked as a barista at a Swedish coffee shop and rented an apartment so loud from the passing subway that he could practice his sax all day long without disrupting anyone—and Sweden, where he's moving to be with his Swedish girlfriend and hopefully make a living as a musician. Jack and I have long been engaged in a competition to see who can pursue the least lucrative creative career in the most far-flung place, and he is now winning. We have reached a pinnacle of impoverished-artist seekerhood at this moment, Jack holed up in the barn with his sax and me in the cabin with my gestating baby, my parents surely damning our hippie arts education.

We refer to Jack's repetitious sequence of scales on the baritone sax as his fart noises. "Makin' my fart noises on the bari," he says, and then goes through a range I label from popcorn to cauliflower to maple-'n'-onion baked beans. He cracks the screen door, opens a little valve on the bari, and dumps his spit. I sit on the front porch and write the small details of passing time, for lack of anything else to write, for lack of a self or story to layer on it all. Dad in the garden planting tomatoes. A ruby-throated hummingbird coming to taste the snapdragons. Dad and Jorge struggling with the drunken careening of the wheelbarrow. A blacksnake in the grass. The mowers going again in our neighbor Dotty's pastures, marking the start of long summer evenings. A luna moth, with its ornate, ersatz, unseeing eyes. Jorge imitating a giant squid, lurching toward me with arm-tentacles. Rain that starts across the valley, the sound of a whisper heard from another room, and moves closer in a white veil until it is thrashing the cabin. It gushes from the rutted roof and is gone, off tittering in the woods. I realize I have never before watched it move.

I remember the night I spent with my grandma when she was in hospice, dying; how after I'd calmed my crying and laid down my book, I came into a fragile awareness that lasted from that moment through her death and for a few days afterward. It was of the naked world, the empty world, beneath the banal everyday, beneath all the assumptions and plans we take for granted, all the fictions we assiduously maintain. Nothing mattered and yet everything was vivid, equalized. Part of the task of the self is to organize the world into hierarchies, tiers of relationships and preferences and desired outcomes and shoulds. But death levels all that, and we are left with a cup of coffee, boxes of trinkets, the green lichens on bare branches, pizza. There is an ache and a rawness in each conversation, each landscape. Sifting through a shoebox of Jesus key chains, summiting a wild peak, welcoming an adoring audience of literary hipsters: all take on the same sheen of meaninglessness that begs a search for deeper meaning.

In pregnancy, an experience whose shifts parallel those of grief, I find myself once again shaken by this awareness. Nothing matters, and I have long been a person for whom things *matter*.

I do not know how not to want, as wanting seems an

essential precursor to the societal mandate of getting: book contracts, jobs, fame, from point A to point B.

What does your character want? goes the refrain in a fiction workshop. This wanting, and the various barriers to its fulfillment, are what drive a story. Without wanting the character is lifeless, the plot rudderless. The reader has no motivation to keep reading. Without want I cannot plan, practice, prepare, measure. Without wanting and obtaining, wanting and losing and wanting more feverishly, moving always closer to and farther from an ideal vanishing point, there is nothing to save me from sinking into insignificance, banality, and smallness, from being consumed by the dogged tedium of the everyday.

So there is nothing left to do but recognize that insignificance, banality, smallness, are all there is; they come sprouting up through the loam of pregnancy, bare as the first green shoots in the hot boxes. Jorge holds out a shoe to show me a tiny frog huddled inside. "Poor stinky *rana*," he says. Jorge plays corn hole by himself, the bags hitting the board in a steady *thud, thud, thud*. A heron flies over the pastures holding a fish in its mouth. For the first time in my life I notice the creeping return of shade under the trees. Jack emerges from the barn with a cup of coffee in hand, his eyes crinkled against the sun. I hold up Suzuki's *Not Always So* in greeting. "'Sup, Shunryu?" he asks. "Whatcha realizin' today?"

"We don't seek for anything," Suzuki writes, "because when we seek for something, an idea of self is involved.

Then we try to achieve something to further the idea of self." To seek, to expect, to want, are to enter into a cycle of perpetually seeking, expecting, and wanting, digging further and further into the narrow burrow of the self. What is achieved is small, fleeting, insignificant, and never enough. It flakes away the instant we are confronted with birth or death. All of my attempts at design pale in comparison to just letting go, but letting go is terrifying, and I must do it again and again. Without the self, maintained and defined by wanting, there is nothing to separate me from the world.

Jorge and I go for a walk in the pastures after sunset. The sky is a darkening blue. Over the woods and grasses lingers a pale mist, into which the huge moon fizzes off-white. All the acute desire that has defined my adult life—of jobs and accolades and adventures—is absorbed by prayer. "What is holy—that's all I want to know," writes the poet Carrie Fountain. In the front pasture Jorge makes me stop for a picture. He perches the tripod uphill, where it takes in pregnant me and the apple orchard and the grasses that slope toward the valley's center. Far behind us in my parents' house, the TV lights up, bright images against the impending dark. Jorge presses the trigger and then sprints downhill through the wet grasses to place the flash. There is silence, stillness, a flare of light. He does this again and again, and I close my eyes and pray, slowly, carefully, as I've learned to do this year. The year I learned to pray.

We spend maybe twenty minutes on photos before Jorge is happy with one, on his screen a little blue moonlit representation of our blue moonlit scene. We continue into the back pasture, where we can see the moon in full glory above the ridge. It has the sandy color and regal fatigue of an old lion. I roam to the edge of the farthest pasture to where I can hear the creek running: a different sound in darkness, furtive and self-possessed. The inversion of night makes a new landscape of the familiar. I turn left and rise past the persimmon tree into the open field, the trees aproned by the soft gray shade of moonlight, their leaves shimmering in night breeze. I pray for myself to become a mother, this role I want to inhabit in the coming year. I pray to come into a different self: fuller, calmer, more compassionate. I pray. And then I look to a star, the only one visible in the back pasture, and pray for Elena, for my baby, her above all else, and nothing else matters. We return through the quiet slippery pools of mud between pastures, and I feel myself only as prayer, my whole body keeling toward the birth of this new being. I am erased, I am singing. John Cage writes, "Everybody has a song which is no song at all—it is a process of singing, and when you sing, you are where you are."

During the most annihilating, intense pain of my life, I am expected to breathe deeply and open myself, like a tulip. In birthing classes the nurse warns us that she's seen many women who wanted to do natural childbirth clamp up with anxiety at the pain and end up needing analgesics or an epidural.

The pain starts at 1:00 a.m. on June 4, and at first, it's a curiosity. I actually think, *Oh, so this is what a painful contraction feels like.* The pain is unlike the low swampy throb of period cramps, unlike a bellyache. It radiates, starting at a center point and then undulating outward like the rays on a sketched sun, before those rays turn back and clench down on my whole torso for an excruciating five to ten seconds. It is still an exciting novelty while I stuff granola bars in a duffel bag, while we climb into the Honda in the thick of night and start with a crunch down the gravel drive, giddy nervousness giving me goose bumps. Heavy fog shawls the pastures, and the fireflies shine through it like bioluminescence. From here onward, every time I see fireflies I will think of this night, will remember the wing of the car door open in the driveway, the pulse of gold through the mist, the pain and the brink. Stepping off the cabin porch, easing my animate belly into the front seat, I have a vertiginous sense of the threshold: when I return, I will have a baby, the wormhole to this life of pregnancy and preparenthood will have finally closed completely.

On the two-hour drive into the hospital, in the triage room, and even making my way down the hall to the delivery room, I can separate myself from the pain, see it at a distance. Its intensity is observed and noted. In fact, I note that my sharp, ragged breaths and long shuddering exhales sound exactly like my grandmother's when she was dying.

I suck on a purple Popsicle and then have to go to the bathroom immediately to expel it; Meg shows up, touches my belly, and hugs me; Mom shows up and hands me a black-and-white cloth box with a stuffed bunny and a monkey rattle and onesies; my sister takes blurry pictures of my face raw with emotion; and Jorge, as he does, weathers it all grinning and letting me squeeze the life out of his hand from time to time. There is laughter, banter, little waxy cups of water.

But shortly after we enter the delivery room, Mom and my sister and Meg and Jorge and bent, shuffling me arriving in a happy pack with the midwife and the nurse, there is a shift. The last thing I remember thinking is *How in the world did my sister compare this to running a marathon?* I half laugh, and then am swept under. The pain takes me like a riptide and leaves only the barest shred of conscious experience. I double over, clutch at myself. I clench my teeth and my muscles. I bark "Ow-ow-ow-ow-ow!" involuntarily, as if the words are being yanked from me like flopping fish from water. The midwife says, "Say 'open.' Not 'ow.' 'Open.'" Desperate, I say it, "Open, open, open." Each time it comes out a little calmer than the last, the *o* sound releasing breath. I breathe audibly, slowly, through the contractions.

They measure me, and my dilation is four centimeters: the same as when I arrived. At this moment I understand that I must make my peace with labor, or I'll never make it. I strip down to a bikini, shuffle doubled over to the bathroom with the birthing ball, and keel over said ball in the shower for the next three hours, rocking and moaning. In these hours I am nothing but pain and a vessel. I close my eyes and envision riding the contractions like waves, rising in increasing pain to the searing crest, holding there with forced breathing for the ten or fifteen seconds of peak intensity, then breathing my way down as they recede. Jorge's jeans are rolled up at the ankles, and his bare, brown feet are the only thing I see. They are tender and beautiful even in this agony; I notice and remember this. I open.

I move into transition and the contractions become unbearable; I stumble to the bed, lie on my side, and kick, screaming, "Ow-ow-ow!" like machine-gun fire. I am at this moment seeing only snippets of faces, hearing my sister say, "You're doing so good," and Jorge saying, "You're doing amazing." The midwife asks if I want to start pushing. I say yes, not really hearing my own voice, and then I am pushing my feet against my sister and Jorge's palms with all my strength. I begin to shout, guttural primeval sounds, over and over, which feels good. The midwife interrupts: "Sarah," she says, "you can roar your baby out. But right now you're not doing any work. You have to bear down." I've been evading the pain with all my noise.

I am silent, internalizing all that energy, and then I bear down. For the first time I feel an enormous wall of pressure, a discomfort unlike anything I've experienced, as I try to free this other body from my own through a very small space. I bear down until it seems I am near exploding. When each contraction ends, some meager sliver of self-awareness returns, and I pant, cry a little, then feel the building of another contraction and bear down again. At some point I wail, "I can't do this anymore!" and Meg leans in and says, "You are doing it." I bear down again. And again.

"Look at all that hair!"

And a cry, and there is a head with full black hair. One more push, and she is out, incarnadine and screaming. The midwife raises her quickly to my chest and I am in shock, half laughing, saying, "My baby, my baby," as she looks up at me with dark eyes. I am surprised at their darkness, their differentness from my own. They are little shimmering opals. She is wet and ruddy and completely herself, and I am ecstatic, startled, touching her tiny hands and feet. It is 2:51 p.m. Outside, it is raining.

It is not until a few weeks after the birth, when I am fully immersed in milk and sun and poo, summer and new motherhood, that I see this is what I've been trying to do all along: open, open, open. The shedding of self is painful. The urge is to seize up against it, hold tighter and tighter to the old givens, but eventually it will only get harder and harder, the passageway narrower and narrower. Instead I have to let go: open. Open above all to not knowing who I am, where I'm going.

On the top of a mountain in New York I lie under a muslin swaddle and look into my baby's eyes. It is the longest she and I have stared at each other, and the first time I sense real seeing and intent from her. Her eyes are big and dark, fringed with her father's lush lashes. Beyond the blanket is a navy sky, an overcast day. My baby is taking in the world, taking in me in front of her. I look into her eyes and feel myself absorbed by her like one liquid poured into another. Her eyes search mine under that frail porous muslin, which turns the harsh mountain sunlight to soft heat. Mother and daughter. *Madre y hija.* A self feels a terribly flimsy and frivolous thing, a ridiculous concept to entertain or mourn. I am a being in the world, an animal. I merge with this small, plump brown body, its wide imploring eyes in which the act of living is direct, urgent, like a river. In which there is nothing to do but live.

Motherhood for me washes away my imagined significance and reveals a clear and terrifying stillness beneath. "When you have this kind of genuine connection with yourself and your world," Suzuki writes, "you may begin to encounter wakefulness. You suddenly feel as if you're in a vast, wide-open space with unlimited breathing room. It's as if you've stepped out of a small, dark, stuffy tent and found yourself standing on the rim of the Grand Canyon. This is the place of just being. It's not an otherworldly, ethereal place. You haven't transcended the ordinary details of your life. Quite the opposite. You've finally contacted them 100 percent."

I am in the kitchen cooking spaghetti Bolognese in syrupy August light. From everywhere comes the sizzle and pulse of crickets, their insistency in this final luxe of heat. The pastures are colored in the early autumn palate of Queen Anne's lace, coneflowers, Day-Glo butterfly weed. The sauce is puckering on the stove, the baby is in her Björn bouncer, and I think, *I should put on music, I should listen to a podcast,* that old urge to make this time useful, to justify it. But in this period after the birth, for months, I don't want to listen to music. I don't want to listen to podcasts. I don't want any layers on top of what is right now. I have descended from the world of abstractions, from life lived in a gaseous ring above the everyday, to the yogurty ripeness of baby shit, the grappling of pudgy fingers, the slow sand-dune slide into afternoon sleep. I've found a way of being that isn't looking for explanation or stimulation or a way out. After these years of nonstop stressing about being smart and successful, padding and feeding and listening to the self, I am in a realm where all that matters is this creaking wooden rocker putting her to sleep. All I want to do is be good to this small, new human being. It is a meditation, a prayer, a daily practice.

For the first six weeks of the baby's life, I tend to her in this timeless, absorbing fever. Occasionally I glance at the clock and register the time as if it were a passing cloud: 2:15, 7:32, 1:15, 6:45. The days lap, one over the other, and like the baby I note changing textures and temperatures, inside and outside, light and dark, but I do not inhabit or control but rather am passing time. This unthinking immersion is satisfying: a feeling of wholeness, rightness, I've sought my entire life. I can and want to do only this one thing; it is what I was made for. In this sense of absorption and completeness, I exist in a separate space from the rest of the world, or am not clamoring for position in the world in the way I was before. It's the closest I've come to having a calling. In my career I've never been able to claim a divine selection: *Oh, I've known since I was three years old that I was going to be a writer!* But for a brief instant motherhood consumes me and I relish this singularity of purpose.

Yet the initial timeless fever of tending to her tames, and I begin to discern blocks of time—a half hour while she naps, fifteen minutes while she gazes at trees and birds—when I can ostensibly "get things done." I answer an email here; I sneak in a few pages in my journal; I spend an entire afternoon in the dark of the upstairs bedroom reading Malcolm Lowry's *Under the Volcano* while Jorge and the baby sleep. The more moments like these I am given or manage to seize the more I sense a fracturing: the tidiness of a clear self, even one wholly defined by and in service to another self, being eroded by the drag of conflicting desires and goals. I try to finish reading a poem before I respond to her whimpers and feel a guilt frighteningly disproportionate to her brief fidgeting. I put down *Under the Volcano* to walk her around for twenty minutes while she falls back to sleep, then put it down again ten minutes later when she wakes, then again ten minutes later when she wakes again, and I am appalled to find resentment where before there was a beatific sense of duty.

I try to tamp down the growing lust for these moments apart from her and the conflicting emotions they stir; I have found clarity and am reluctant to forfeit it. I want to feel a singing purity while baking oatmeal cookies and building block castles. In spite of all the thinking I have done about the fiction of self, I can't help but fall for its illusion once again: this self a Mother, who consumes the traveler of the previous decades as neatly as a big fish swallowing a smaller one.

Damn it. The baby is crying. I am midsentence in *Under the Volcano,* the prose is rapturous, I am in writerly bliss but *yes*. Yes, here I come. *Yes!* I am a writer, I am a mother, I am carrying her through the plush August afternoon.

These selves, the traveler and the writer and the

mother, do not fold together into one, are not mirrored on and on identically in a harmonic chord. Often they are in direct contradiction. I discover this on our first visit to Mexico with the baby. We've invited friends to our apartment for drinks. The baby grows fussy, and I take her into the bedroom to put her to sleep, but she won't go down for the night. She steadies, her breathing calms, and then just as I begin to creep away, she startles and cries. After a half hour or so of this I grow frustrated, listening to the muted party sounds outside. *Why tonight, of all nights?* I think. She fidgets and whimpers and I become increasingly impatient. And then out of my familiar impatience, that characteristic itch I've carried with me through many situations on many continents, emerges another self, a ghost slipping out of my body: the mother. She has been in me all along and only in this moment can I feel her, watch her. The old me is still there, but she is watching in awe as another self holds and gently rocks the baby. I have cleaved in two, and all the while a third self—perhaps that essential core self of which Buddhism speaks, who simply observes fleeting emotions and desires as they flash around her like heat lightning— looks on. The mother whispers soothing words, rocks, loves, laughs at the other impatient foot-stomping self, and forgives her as one forgives a recalcitrant child, while the other self thinks, *Fucking a, fucking a, how I miss that life of mezcal with abandon,* while the third watches the whole process unfold. And then the baby falls asleep, and all those selves evaporate as quickly as they'd appeared. I rejoin my friends drinking beer at the kitchen table; the lights of distant colonias bristle on the far hill.

"Without losing yourself by sticking to a particular rule or understanding, keep finding yourself, moment, after moment," Suzuki writes. I am on the porch rocking, the fully leaved maples on the driveway a swishing chorus, the baby's slow-fluttering lids speaking of sleep. My eyes meet Little Dude's sad mutt mug, she gives an exaggerated groan of neglect and chomps at a fly, and I am a task, a role, more than a person, a mother rocking, Sarah, yes, but Sarah sounds absurd, like calling myself Queen Fantasia the Fifteenth. I rock, rock, rock in time and space, Little Dude's absurdly long purple tongue stuck out in a big yawn, the grass a glowing aura of green, a solitary finch perched on the highest branch of the apple tree.

In July, the baby and I avidly follow the World Cup. Germany beats Argentina in the final, despite my frenetic cheering for the latter in the name of Latin American solidarity. Shortly after the game it grows dark and windy and then storms in that frothy, full-on way it does here in the Midwest, as if a smoky-browed stranger has just swept in through the door and held the whole scene in thrall. I am on the porch with the baby, and she is fussy. I nurse, press her to my chest, and when that doesn't work hold her out in front of me, her head in my hands. Like this I rock her, watching her eyes blink slowly open and shut, watching her stare at me, the rain, the world on this stormy summer afternoon. I hold her toward the cabin, its cozy yellow interior, the rain pounding down white and silver behind me and sending up a fury of spray from the grass. As it lessens I turn her toward the storm, and I see that this is the whole of motherhood: that slow turn outward, facing the rain, the drops on the hostas, the broken fence beam, the coneflowers and the butterfly weed, the woods, the pastures, the thrashing sky.

Farm summer is blurred in infinite shades of green and yellow—chamomile and lime, emerald and daffodil—bound by the bathlike midwestern heat. Amid this green and yellow mugginess I dance one afternoon with the baby to Jack's version of "Caribbean Fire Dance." I am ecstatic to be getting a tune in lieu of fart noises, and Jack is letting loose with it, practicing for an upcoming solo show. I strut the baby around the yard through falling walnut leaves. I get all caught up in the dancing and the day, and when it is done, I applaud.

"Bravo, little man, bravo!" I hoist the baby as if she were a Grammy.

"Thanks, dude," comes the winded call from the dark recesses of the barn.

Not long after, we all go to Columbus to see Jack play

at a small bar selling artisanal mead. There are the requisite hipsters and tattooed bartenders and a few self-conscious girls who lurk near the edges of the stage, clutching drinks, while I give them the big-sister narrow-eye from the bar. Jack begins to play and goes through nearly three-fourths of his repertoire before he gets to what I immediately recognize as "Caribbean Fire Dance." The baby is asleep in her sling on my chest and I am rocking back and forth like a small craft at sea, in the way new parents do for months on end without thinking. Jack's face is wrought and red and immersed in the song, sweat streaming into his ginger Viking beard. I think of him in the barn, working his way up the fart scale and then busting out with an "Oh, fuck! Yeah, that's it!" in adorable earnestness. I think of his spit dumpage, of his deep-in-thought face when he steps out of the barn with coffee mug in hand, catches me watching him, and asks with a grin, "How're the goos goin'?"

Now he is onstage pouring himself into the vessel of his horn, his whole self given over to that wail and treble like I give myself to a story. I feel that heart-gut emptying, all of one's brief human life channeled into this tenuous expression on a Thursday evening before a crowd of dudes in wry-sloganed tees shouting, "Yo Brian, hit me up with a Dos Equis!" I want to slap these oblivious people who flit in and out from the patio, pawing at each other in rompers and Vans without socks, I want to dash their ten-dollar habañero mead margaritas to the refinished concrete floor and say, *Do you see that breathless wonder up there?!* I feel for Jack, the red pinch of his face and the windedness of trying so hard, channeling himself into each note, pushing himself up and down the scales, and straining to swing between high and low, light and dark, on the boughs of the heart. *Little red beard,* I find myself thinking, *it's so hard, and so thankless, and so you have to try like you do, try with the dedication of ritual and the acceptance of tedium, try through all the everyday banality of the fart noises, and you also have to give up, recognize that everyone will walk back and forth in front of your stage thinking about the fat content of organic tofu burgers. You play on anyway, free from the need for validation, from the division between practice and performance, barn solo and bar solo.*

I am obviously speaking to myself as much as my little brother, learning that the work does not mean much, might not matter at all, if it is not equally worthwhile for a two-month-old on a farm in rural Ohio or an auditorium of aficionados at Carnegie Hall. This may be utopic, but it is also essential to one's sanity as an artist, to making anything of depth, to pushing beyond the everyday struggles of ego and success that only grow more elusive and crazy making.

"When we are trying to be active and special and to accomplish something," Suzuki writes, "we cannot express ourselves. Small self will be expressed, but big self will not appear from the emptiness. From the emptiness only great self appears."

• • •

For my thirty-second birthday, just over a month after I give birth, my parents make me dinner. Meg makes beef curry, and Dad makes a cucumber-pepper salad and dal, and we have birthday cake, white with three candles. They sing "Happy Birthday" while I hold a sleeping Elena to my chest. When they say "Dear Sar-ah" I feel their tenderness as parents anew, seeing me as a daughter and a mother, a daughter who will always be such, even to their deaths, and now a mother who is beginning to understand why. Their gentleness is not only for me, but also for the experience of once having rocked a baby to sleep, having once begun and now watching that beginning again. I feel for the first time my own life in the ongoing pitch of lives. I can feel myself passing the torch in thirty years, making beef curry, blowing out the candles, and then being gone, and on and on.

I think of my dad hiking in the snow, calling "No bunnies!" to his dog Rosie when she runs off on a scent. He looks grizzled and sweet in the gray winter afternoon; he tells me, "There are only so many more times I can fall off a horse." While I am on the porch feeding the baby, he walks past with his little camp chair and his man purse and waves; he is going to write in his journal by the creek. I find him one afternoon with the baby, sitting in a rocking chair on the edge of the pastures. She is fast asleep on his chest, a deep heavy sleep from which she is not easily roused. He's wearing a leather hat and watching the day's soft elision into dusk, the birds flitting from birdhouse to birdhouse. He is feeling again the weight of a baby's trusting body, the tiny gusts of her breath.

Not long after, I am on the front porch of the house with Jack and his girlfriend, Sofia, holding the baby, watching another storm roll in. A huge triangular mass of gray cloud is advancing, the wind is picking up speed in the trees, and then the storm cracks open: thunder, thrashing of leaves, rain. Silver sheets pummel the grass and garden. Our voices are drowned out. The storm does its work in oceanic navy light, as if we were under the belly of a ship. Fifteen minutes later, it is over. The ship moves on, and in its place shines a landscape of sharp, sublime contrast. The sky is a patchwork of empires: battleship gray, gold, cerulean. Over the woods, a double rainbow appears. Beneath it, the pastures glow with heavy light thick as lacquer. The farm is quiet. Sofia and Jack are making gin and tonics in the kitchen, and Dad and I are in the yard with the baby. It is still raining, just enough to wet the baby's face.

I see now the object of Dad's life has been to create this safe space: the front porch in the midst of a storm, the comforting white noise of Jack and Sofia puttering about in the kitchen, and I understand the meaning of family. I see myself as only part of a cycle, which unfolds in this place he has built. The place is as much himself, the rock of himself upon which we engrave ourselves, as it is this patch of Ohio.

I remember in the previous fall, in the dark of my uncertainty about the pregnancy, going on a walk with Jorge and my dad in late afternoon, just before dusk. We climbed slowly through the lycopodiums to a rocky shelf that overlooks the woods and the valley beyond them. The light was that combination of ice blue and copper particular to clear days in early winter. It came slanting at a low angle through the beeches and warmed the green moss on boulders. Dad and Jorge were talking about trail building, and I had the sense of being in an eternal scene, like the specifics of conversation didn't matter and there was just that moment spread over the whole of my lifetime. The Ohio landscape seemed as essential a part of me as an eye or an organ; its rainbow of greens, its winter skies, are all that remain below the myriad ongoing definitions and assumptions that snag and then drift away. If there is any self I can claim, it is only the fleeting feeling of recognition in these woods, of walking through them behind the tall redheaded comfort of my father. Elena will hold something else, a snatch of bawdy street fair in Mexico and perhaps California pine and always the stellar brilliance of fireflies in early Ohio summer; elements she will absorb beyond whomever she dreams and creates herself to be. I see the smallness of my own life in this place, this center, the aerie of family and the newly wet hills. I see myself as only the Ohio woods, the light, observed. As Annie Dillard writes, "When everything else has gone from my brain—the President's name, the state capitals, the neighborhoods where I lived, and then my own name and what it was on earth I sought, and then at length the faces of my friends, and finally the faces of my family—when all this has dissolved, what will be left, I believe, is topology: the dreaming memory of land as it lay this way and that."

The summer slants toward fall.

One evening like any other, in late August, there is a rainbow. It is rainbow weather, with the trees spinning silver and schools of yellowing leaves twirling downstream into the thick grasses. All of my pregnancy, and this whole summer of new motherhood, have been rainbow weather: gray and butter yellow, Technicolor blue and electric green, slate and cotton white, rainy and sunny and stormy and calm. The trees tilt with the wind. As I watch, a flock of birds goes wheeling through the eastern sky. When they shift southward, all spinning in formation, they catch the light spilling from behind a cloud, and they all turn silver, a dozen silver coins tossed into the changing sky. Like that they stay an instant, glinting light, incredible, and then again they are birds twirling up and away. A rainbow appears, and then a double. We go out to play cornhole while the day's final clouds ham it up on a blue horizon.

It takes years to really notice this, understand it: the rhythms of a place, the way the sun moves across valley and farm. One afternoon I think of that plan I had in early pregnancy to become a better person: Have I? It is getting close to that reckoning time, nearly three months after the birth. Rocking the baby to sleep on the front porch, I come to see that in pursuit of that question I've stumbled onto something so much bigger, almost so big as to render the earlier question moot. I've stumbled upon, as Suzuki puts it, "the question that is the ground or basis of all answers." Perhaps in some small ways I have become "better"—better at openness, better at quieting the blather and the urge to smear myself across the world in words, personality, opinions. The change is not complete; it jogs back and forth, and I can only be more aware. But the bigger point isn't better personhood, like a task to be accomplished. It isn't a remodeling so I come out on the other side with everyone remarking on my transformation: *You're you, but better!* It's more as if the world has begun to move from the stillness of my limited perspective and become once again a mystery, and the me within it is no longer definable by characteristics, words, or images, no longer the essential core around which the world pivots. At times I have the courage not to need that core, and at times, still, I cling to it.

On our trip to Mexico, we travel the bumpy hour and a half over mountain roads from Oaxaca City to Guelatao to introduce the baby to Jorge's mother. Elena Rosa, we say, meet Rosa, and Jorge's mother laughs her characteristic raspy, deep, humble laugh that embraces all absurdity, especially this small, bundled, black-haired being who shares her name. She exclaims over Elena, strokes her hair, coos at her, wraps her in a shawl with one simple motion I am unable to replicate no matter how patiently I am taught. Rosa sits beside me on her wooden bench overlooking the village and the piney mountains of Oaxaca. She watches me hold the baby and says, *"Una mujer completa."* A whole woman. I know she means that motherhood has filled some gap in me, and I know this is a traditional notion and one women have rightfully fought hard to debunk. But I think of the writer Courtney Martin's definition of the whole self as a radical challenge to the singular, mimetic selves we so often limit ourselves to, both online and in the everyday, the selves who rely on one word or expectation or pattern of behavior. The whole self is irreducible, incongruous, and perpetually unfinished; it is the struggle between contradictions. We try for equilibrium like the tongue of a scale flicking back and forth until it settles, quivering, in a revelatory moment of poise. In this moment we accept all those contradictions and what they say about our becoming, and we possess a rare grace.

At the farm in early September I wake from a nap in the hammock, my mind still coated with that thin furze of disorientation following sleep. Jorge and the baby are in the yard, and the afternoon is bright with clouds like fluffed pillows. Jorge has bought a new mountain bike and urges me to try it. He walks the baby while I curve around the gravel drive. Once I am on the paved road I pump and pump and then sail, legs splayed, wind lifting my hair, the yellow center line undulating up and over the Ohio hills past goldenrod, past the pastures out of which explode bright yellow finches. I think, *I've made it.* The last time I was on this road alone, I stopped, capped knees with sweaty palms, and sobbed, and now here I am—I made it. And here on the other side I see it's still life, still the day to day, the thrill and novelty buffered once again by the slowness of the quotidian.

Nonetheless, when I head back in the cooling afternoon, I want to believe I am a different woman, renewed, changed . . . at least until I pull back into the gravel drive to my husband holding the baby, and I take her in my arms and remember it doesn't much matter. The trembling aspens clatter in a breeze above the driveway. There is no mail. The next morning, the baby wakes herself up, applauding her discovery of applause.

She begins to pay careful attention to our mouths and the words they form, and I practice with her: "Boo," I say, again and again. "Boo," in front of the mirror while she watches, enraptured. The eerie memory of looking at photos of my mother in her thirties comes to me. As a child I remember marveling at how young my mother looked, there on a bridge in Paris, there on a hillside of daffodils. In those pictures she was a person I could never know and who would only ever exist for me as a potent mystery. I think of Elena looking back and seeing me as a young mother, looking in awe at the mystery of who I was, with my braided hair and my checked shirt on the farm in those in-between years of early motherhood. I see my life already gone by. Between one "Boo" and another in the bathroom mirror, my whole life passes.

THE MILK CAVE

"YOU ARE AN ANIMAL," Jorge tells me. We are in bed. The context is not what you might expect. A baby is latched on to my right breast while the left leaks an opalescent waterfall of milk.

"I'm a mammal," I say. This is about as deep as our conversations get in this first month of parenthood. We are upstairs in what we've dubbed "the milk cave"—the cabin's dim bedroom. I spend the better part of my days here, watching as my baby's eager sucking mouth goes rooting and then latches on with the force of a heavy lid sealed shut on an overflowing container. There is nothing soft or gentle about my baby's latch. It is the precise enactment of its definition: a clamping on, a fastening of two bodies. I feel a sudden tug of suction, a rasp of thirst, then sleepiness. I listen for the *ker, ker, ker* of her swallowing.

Before I gave birth, I knew breastfed babies need to eat every two hours. But knowing this did not prepare me for the sheer amount of time breastfeeding demands. Even if someone had told me, "Twenty minutes per breast per feeding," it would still have taken sitting down every two hours for forty minutes for me to understand, because just like every other aspect of pregnancy and motherhood—morning sickness, contractions—the imagined experience turns out to be laughably unlike the experience itself.

I am hunkered down in the milk cave in a mess of sheets, sticky with an overabundance of milk, balancing the baby in the football hold and watching her eyes blink slowly open and closed with the rhythm of sucking. I finally finish, set her in her Björn bouncer, and start digging into emails, and then, again, she shoves her fist in her mouth and starts smacking her gums with comic eagerness.

Whole yellow and green summer days slip by between the milk cave and the breezy porch, gazing at baby on the breast, at the whirring fan and the sheets with their pattern of roses, at the pastures of wavering grasses incandescent in afternoon light. Nights I awake at two, at four, at six, and in the grainy coffee black I hold the warm parcel of her, feel the eager pressure of those small gums, our animal bodies pressed together, the darkness undulating a bit in my delirium. I try not to fall asleep, have half thoughts, then enter a space of no thoughts at all.

At first the novelty of the experience is enough to consume me entirely. But after a few weeks, I grow restless. I have to do something else. Or rather, I have to *do* something, since breastfeeding somehow doesn't count. It seems to exist in that nowhere realm of feminine activity: in the back stairways, the dark kitchens, those places where women do the invisible work that drives and maintains life. The essential ground-level work: the feeding, the nurturing, the staving off of chaos, work not measured in hours, miles, words, or dollars. Work that doesn't count as such. I sit and stare and enter an oxytocin-fueled dream state, a new kind of boredom.

In the past, I've felt boredom as a restrained and tedious anticipation: how many more minutes in the waiting room, or until the bus arrives, or until this lecturer stops droning on. Boredom as a toe-tapping impatience for the next event. But in breastfeeding boredom is a kind of presence, an altered way of being. It doesn't involve any anticipation. The act of giving milk itself is pleasant and soothing; it's not that I am eager for it to end. And it's not that it is uninteresting, between the strange palpable effects of the oxytocin and the mesmerizing face of the latched baby. It just doesn't fit into the matrix of productivity or purpose or attention I'm accustomed to. It is simply being, a mammal animal being, layered with a human consciousness as thin and light as linen. It is not directed, not overtly constructive, and while it may spark curiosity or desire, it may also leave the mind unperturbed by either. There could be a revelation, an insight to be used in an essay or a dinner conversation, or there could be nothing more than the vaguest drifting of consciousness among the wind in the trees, a faint awareness of the sound the poet Pattiann Rogers describes as a "cavalry of paper horses." It is this lack of drive and intentionality, lack of an actively interpreting self, that I find so unfamiliar and disconcerting. That I call *boredom*.

So I do what we do when we become bored: I buy an iPhone. The iPhone is incomparably handy for traveling and for taking six thousand photos of baby in hooded bath towels, baby in socks, baby in sweatpants, baby with flowers, baby with dogs, but breastfeeding is the final justification: I need a task to perform. And so at 2:00 a.m. I start writing one-handed emails, checking Twitter, Googling "Muriel Rukeyser." I get things done. I rejoin the ranks of multitaskers, not only living my life but cataloging and documenting it, too, making sure it adheres to measurable standards of productivity.

It only takes a week or so to recognize the loss behind this gain. The self I've returned to—busy, hyperaware of a particular situation and its particular worth and where she is heading and why—feels more boring than the one present in milk and darkness. I can't fall asleep again at 3:00 a.m. after the constant churning of Twitter. And each time I turn from the screen to my baby's face I feel guilty, as if I've just missed a whole era for the forgettable pseudo-events taking place over and over on the spinning hamster wheel of cyberspace.

One night, as I'm breastfeeding, checking email on my phone, and thinking about this tension between presence and achievement, I come across a recent post highlighting the work of the psychoanalyst Adam Phillips, who emphasizes the importance of boredom in learning to pay attention to the world. Phillips writes: "In boredom . . . there are two assumptions, two impossible options: there is something I desire, and there is nothing I desire. But which of the two assumptions, or beliefs, is disavowed is always ambiguous, and this ambiguity accounts, I think, for the curious paralysis of boredom. . . . In boredom there is the lure of a possible object of desire, and the lure of the escape from desire, of its meaninglessness."

It is this in-between that makes boredom so disconcerting. I'm staring out at the pastures, hypnotic in summer heat, their hazy grasses swaying, lulled by this escape from desire, its meaninglessness, and then a thought comes, and I want equally to follow it and to let it go.

Dad is carrying in his oven-mitted hands a blueberry cobbler Meg has made for us. He sets it on the porch table next to me and the baby. Doughy, sweet steam wafts up. He walks off through the rococo greens of trees and grass and pastures while I nurse the baby and smell the cobbler. It is days after the birth, and I am oozing blood. Down there I am swollen, throbbing. I take a strange pleasure in it, in its reminder of the intensity of birth, of the capabilities of my body. The baby latches, sending a shivery jolt of pain through me. Thin milk spills from her rosebud mouth over her body, which is a deep burgundy. For weeks after her birth she looks like a kidney bean and is covered in a black down, incredibly fine, which I stroke along her tiny arms and back. Her small body is as charged with scent as potpourri; the house is filled with it, sunny hay, and with the redolence of milk, blood, yellow seedy baby poop, the messiness of two humans making it through the first weeks of life. Outside the sky is the faded motley white of sea salt caked on skin.

"For artists or writers to express their direct experience," Suzuki writes, "they may paint or write. But if their experience is very strong and pure, they may give up trying to describe it: 'Oh my.' That is all."

In July, we slaughter the roosters. Meg had ordered eight chicks in the spring, and we'd discovered shortly after their arrival that two were in fact roosters, who soon began to fight with each other and abuse the poor hens. Meg and Dad decide they'll have to be culled, and the day comes when Elena is just over a month old. Dad makes his long strides up to the cabin in muck boots, stopping to check on the irises, and calls a hello into our cavern of strewn diapers and books and glasses of water.

Dad and Jorge catch the roosters, and then Dad, Jorge, Jack, and me—baby snugged to my chest—proceed in drenching heat to the boat shed near the horse barn, where Dad has set out a little weather-beaten table with blue legs. Atop it lies a hatchet. While Dad gets ready, Jack holds the first rooster, and Jorge walks the second a short distance away so it won't witness the slaughter of its compadre. The smaller rooster in Jack's arms is already scraggly and raw from being attacked by the larger one.

"Are you okay, dude?" Dad asks Jack, who looks uneasy. Jack nods. Above us the sky is a hot deep blue fleeced with cottontail clouds. It is the peak of afternoon, and the light is direct, poured yellow from above as if from a pitcher. Jack brings the rooster to the table and presses its neck to the worn wood. I am carrying sleeping Elena in a cotton sling. Her face is soft and round, sweat pearling on her precious nose, her tiny strawberry tongue white with milk. The heat settles around us all, watery, undulating.

With the front pasture rising ripe green behind him, Dad raises the hatchet and brings it down with a rubbery crack, severing the head in one clean blow. Blood geysers from the neck and sprays all over Jack, who half mutters and half cries, "Oh, man, oh, man, oh, man." Dad grabs a bucket and says, "Here, dude," and Jack thrusts the gurgling body into it neck down. Rooster feet stick up, spindly and yellow, still twitching. On the table, in the head, one green eye blinks. "Oh, man, oh, man," the dude says. He is polka-dotted with blood. His farm baptism, we joke later.

Then it is Jorge's turn. Having grown up in the mountains of Oaxaca and attended an agricultural high school, he is familiar with animals and their harvesting. He has made his own chorizo, hunted rabbit, watched his mom swiftly kill their chickens and boil them for *mole amarillo*. He emerges from beside the barn with the second rooster, carefully positions its neck at table's edge, and smack comes the hatchet, the head now a writhing absurdity, the body a feathered cavity fountaining blood. Jorge ducks the body quickly in the bucket to drain, sparing himself any spray. Elena sleeps.

"Whoo boy," Dad says. He takes the first body out and begins cleaning it, pulling the feathers from the still-warm skin with a soft ripping sound. I see the black points at the feathers' tips, the black dimples on the skin where each fit so precisely. Dad carves the meat from the bone and the bone from the body. The breasts are measly and muscled, and Dad lays them on a platter on which is depicted a bucolic farm scene. He whittles elegantly around the lurid jumble of organs, chops off the feet, and tosses them with the feathers into the bucket. I stand in the boathouse shade with Elena, who is deep in that beatific newborn sleep, her cheeks rouged, her eyelashes a fine-tooth comb, her breaths an almost imperceptible heat among the greater forceful heat of the day. Once Dad finishes we walk back up the hill toward the house with a platter of meat and a bucket of feathers. I stoop to pick a four-leaf clover. That night, we eat the tough grilled meat with barbecue sauce and suck at buttery corn on the cob while the chickens bumble around the grass, the sunflowers bowing above them like monks.

• • •

Dad is building what will soon come to be known as the Pagan Sculpture. He has harvested gnarled tree roots and old gray logs, a few stolid trunks, and a heap of classic John Menkedick miscellanea, and it all sits in the front pasture awaiting transformation. Every day he goes out to work on it, waving a gloved hand at me on the porch. Slowly it gains a base, then rises into pyramidal form, with the roots like Medusas tentacling out from the sides. We are called to consult from time to time about the positioning of a particular piece: does it flow or interrupt from this angle, will we trip over it if he leaves it down here? Finally, one evening when Jorge and the baby and I are sitting on Meg and Dad's porch, watching blue take over from the wet yellow heat, he comes striding up and declares it done.

To our credit, Jorge and I last through dinner and several glasses of wine before I say, after assuring him that it is superinteresting and unusual, that actually, um, it sort of reminds us of a TV show we've been watching. What show? *True Detective*. The Satan worshipper totems favored by its backwoods serial killer bear an unfortunate, striking resemblance to the Pagan Sculpture. Dad has never heard of *True Detective* but sports a rueful smile and offers that maybe we should bury the placenta—still sitting in a white tub in his freezer—out there. This leads to a summerlong succession of sacrifice jokes, while the Pagan Sculpture slowly gathers the farm around itself.

Dad channeled some sort of energy into it, his mysterious Dad force, for every day I walk the baby out to it and stroke its sides, and when he has her, he does the same. Morning glories, my and Dad's favorite flowers, spiral up the sculpture's triangular sides. The mini-Victrola of each glory is lined with silken fur, a luminescent yellow shining from the center. They twist open every morning with a bright clanging—in Spanish, they are called *rompa platos,* or "plate breakers"—and by afternoon have folded themselves up like parasols. Dad has planted gourds, too, and they dangle in the summery mess of vines, the baby giving a sudden burble of delight when I tease one out.

This, now, is the center of my days, this bewitching, backcountry Ohioan Louvre of uprooted stumps and felled oak; I circumnavigate it with the baby and suspicious Little Dude and regal Leroy, who sprawls himself on its sun-warmed sides as if it were a throne constructed explicitly for his glory. What would I have said three, five, ten years ago had someone told me the touchstone of my life would be an improvised Buddhist heathen sculpture on my dad's Ohio farm?

"Eliminating purpose, awareness increases," writes Suzuki. "Therefore my purpose is to remove purpose."

Boredom is a way of eliminating purpose, and thus can become paradoxically compelling. Robert Gottlieb writes of the paradigm-shifting choreography of Merce Cunningham and John Cage, "It was very boring. Boring was tremendously exciting in the revolution." Cage used boredom to heighten the unheard sounds of the everyday; in his famous composition *4'33"*, there is no conventional "music" to listen to, no artistic composition of the type we're familiar with, only what seems to be silence. Four minutes and thirty-three seconds of very boring silence that requires an altered type of attention—*there is a cough, a sparrow, a siren*—in order to be heard. Had Cage been a woman, perhaps he would have been dismissed entirely, seen as pathetically attempting to elevate the domestic, for it is composed of precisely this type of music. It is the music no one thinks of as such, boring, to be shushed or ignored in the greatness of the true, composed music of the mind.

In *Speak, Memory*, Nabokov writes, "There is, it would seem, in the dimensional scale of the world a kind of deliberate meeting place between imagination and knowledge, a point arrived at by diminishing large things and enlarging small ones, that is intrinsically artistic." Nabokov would surely roll in his grave at the suggestion that this deliberate meeting place is motherhood, and a whole succession of old white literary patriarchs, not to mention much of the current literary elite, would find the assertion that literature could be anything but anathema to motherhood hopelessly sentimental and provincial, quintessential female dottiness. And yet I find literature for the first time here: in the milk cave, in boredom, in the clouds I watch from the porch on days that have no beginning or end. The clouds volcanoes frozen in mid-eruption. The clouds white foam churned up by revelers. The clouds impressionistic smudges of white and navy paint hurriedly roiled with fingertips. The clouds the ragged coat of a snow-white dog on the hunt. The clouds kneaded dough stippled with fingerprints. I find literature in the silence after the baby stops crying, which is unlike any other silence. It is as if the world returns after annihilation and astounds anew with its robins and spaghetti and cut grass. In that moment of abrupt calm there is no good or bad or should or shouldn't, just gratefulness to recognize once again the distant drone of a lawn mower, the tittering gossip of the chickens as they take a wide berth around the dog.

Child-rearing is notoriously boring, monotonous, and repetitive and yet somehow perpetually changing and intermittent; it can be simultaneously frenetic and eternal. Doris Lessing once claimed there is "nothing more boring for an intelligent woman than to spend endless amounts of time with small children," and surely many intelligent women would agree. I might have before I had children. I've spent my life in flight from boredom, seeking to make the most banal experience of brushing my teeth ecstatic by doing it drunk on rice wine in a Chinese train, but moving now between rocking chair and couch and milk cave, switching nipples, whole days passing in a tangle of wet clothes and hair and sheets, I am bored and yet more aware of my life, amazed by it, in awe of my enthrallment to boredom.

I find that I can't operate under the Anglo-Protestant hierarchy that places endeavor, work, intelligence, far above the categories of contemplation, communion, mindfulness. The ultimate shallowness of artistic fervor became terrifyingly clear in pregnancy, and although there are moments when I get my fierce ambition back, its centrality has been forever tested. There is something more, something else, and how it manifests in hours of stroking the smooth arc of a flushed forehead, in making endless slow circles around the pigeons, in saying "treeee" and "dawwwwwg" and "cowwwwww" remains to be told, but I feel obliged to seek it there. The type of meaning making, attention, and purpose necessary for mothering seem far more difficult to master than the concentration and thought I conjure in writing.

One of psychologist Adam Phillips's child subjects explained to him, "When I'm bored, I don't know myself." When I'm not writing, when I'm not multitasking, when I'm not consciously constructing new material, I don't know myself, but I have found that not knowing myself brings its own satisfaction. My sure knowledge now is physical, held within the muscles and tendons that stretched to make room for another body inside mine, that opened to loose it, that strengthen sustaining it.

One night not long after the birth, in my first experience of an out-of-body fatigue that feels like what I imagine an astronaut might suffer if untethered from his spaceship, I crawl upstairs to sleep while Jorge watches

The Good Wife and cradles the baby. I am passed out in otherworldly bliss for some fifteen minutes when I wake up shaking. I shake violently and sweat out what feels like every last ounce of fluid I have in my body. This goes on for an undetermined surreal stretch of time before it finally calms, and, disarmed, I stand and undress. My clothes are drenched. I can wring the sweat from them. Other than standing naked, exhausted, and baffled beside the bed at 8:00 p.m., I feel fine. Not wanting to waste a second of potential sleep on pondering what has just happened, I promptly curl up again and don't wake until the baby is proffered to me some hours later, hungry. Later I find out that my body was ridding itself of all the excess fluid of pregnancy; that in one swift gesture, it released everything it had held so dearly for nine months.

At times in this fragile boredom, I feel like I do when I am backpacking, when the scope of my life has been reduced to what can be carried and enacted in a small patch of woods: light the stove, eat the slop, wash the dishes, start the fire. The basic chores become absorbing, my hands take over from my mind. I am grateful to have gone through the motions of the day, dipped the tin pot in the stream and set it out to dry, laid my aching body down. There is no recourse to the trappings and attractions of the higher mind; a clean face, a nap, a full belly are enough, in the same way that having nursed and rocked and soothed into the comfort of sleep become enough, as satisfying as the most well-wrought paragraph.

In these first few months, the grandeur of the long vista and great expectation are reduced to twenty-minute intervals of panting, fumbling survival. Jorge and I are in a perpetual frenzy of alertness and exhaustion, like animals preparing for winter, if winter came and went every twenty minutes. Our lives are a series of cycles on repeat, with no room for the luxury of anticipation or reflection. We are where we are and we are attempting to extract a poop-soaked onesie with the precision of surgeons so as to not have to give the baby another bath. In ten minutes we'll be in another place entirely: maybe eating cherries and rocking on the front porch to the blue expanse of the pastures at twilight; maybe singing *Bossa Cubana, Bossa Cubana* and bouncing the baby with one foot while simultaneously trying to chop and boil and wash; maybe, blissfully, asleep. The everyday is physical and sensual and immediate and boring, and story is irrelevant before it. We live, to steal Geoff Dyer's description of jazz greats, "as if improvising was a form of clairvoyance."

Life is an endless sequence of tasks, connected only by the huge sky of fish-gill clouds. Running, when I am finally able to do it again; writing, in the few moments I eke out in my journal while she sleeps her newborn sleep of terrifying stillness; reading; driving the two hours into Columbus for towering hot-fudge sundaes with my mom and sister: all possess roughly the same texture and quality as changing the umpteenth diaper of the day, as *shh-shh-shhing* around the pastures, as squinting at the oracle of that tiny scrunched, maybe smiling, maybe squeezing-out-a-fart face. The ability to fantasize about dream lives and to see the day as part of a sweep toward future glory is temporarily lost, and all that is left is the immediate and obvious duty of the moment, with each moment opening out into an entirely new one—peace! frenzy! enchiladas!—and yet all of them ultimately the same. This is boredom, but it is also revelation, it is also a kind of release. Suzuki writes, "When you do something, have a strong air of determination to do it. Woosh! Without any idea of skillful or not, dangerous or not, you just do it. When you do something with this kind of conviction, that is true practice. That is true enlightenment."

There will be no other choice in these first months. I boil peas. I rock until she grows heavy and my eyelids begin to droop. I coo. I press the baby to the breast and pick her up in the dark, I walk her around the wet grass at dawn. I scrub the filthy folds of her chunky little neck. Sometimes I am exhausted and miserable and even angry, and other times I am full of a swooning intensity of love that makes me want to devour her, and others I am laughing a helpless, giddy laugh at the fourth poo in four minutes, but regardless, I fill the tub. I wake up. I hold the small warm body close. All of my previous emotions, taken so seriously, stories in and of themselves, flit across the bedrock of biological determination. I recall Pema Chödrön noting that the average emotion lasts ninety seconds. I recall the old Montana maxim "If you don't like the weather, wait ten minutes." One minute I am swaying her very gently in my outstretched arms, and the next I am reading *Under the Volcano,* and the next I am rubbing Desitin on a teensy bottom. For some women this signifies oppressive, stultifying obligation, and perhaps had someone laid out the mandates of motherhood for me several years ago, I would have agreed. But my expectations haven't aligned with the everyday in which I find myself. For me, this conviction of duty, this barebones necessity of presence, are freeing.

One night she wakes at 3:00 or 4:00 a.m., in that thick gray-black I never really knew until I had a baby, and she rocks on all fours, saying "Ma-ma-ma-ma-ma-ma-ma." She has been learning this in the way babies quietly learn without giving anything away, and now she reveals it with urgency. She must practice. *Ma-ma-ma-ma-ma.* It comes from her as a necessity, from that pure conviction of which Suzuki speaks. It wakes her up. I am ecstatic—*Ma-ma!*—laughing and clapping quietly in the dark, but she is still half asleep, unaware of the thrill her feat has occasioned. She repeats it several more times, exploring the syllables, and then she tumbles over and falls back into a deep sleep.

In motherhood, I discover a surprising physical grace. I have never been good with my hands. By this I don't mean *Oh, I can't hand sew little cat ornaments to gift at birth-*

day parties or *I could never make my baby a homemade dinosaur costume for Halloween.* I mean, I can barely open a bag of cereal. Somehow, there are Cheerios everywhere and the kitchen looks like the scene of a bizarre tragedy and my husband is saying, again, "What is *wrong* with you?"

In the sixth grade, my classmate Sarah Weese used to come over on snow days. By unspoken and unexamined fiat, she and I only hung out when school had been canceled. On these days, we would play Trivial Pursuit and drink the Swiss Miss with the teensy bobby marshmallows and get giddy together in the strange middle-of-the-day quiet of my kitchen. Then we'd go back to school and politely say hello to each other, like travelers who've bonded throughout an epic flight delay but have little in common at their destination.

Even in the sixth grade, Sarah Weese could cut a flawless slice of cheese. At this I marveled. I'd cut irregular gobs like slabs of rock severed in an avalanche. Or the cheese would crumble beneath my knife as if humiliated by my ineptitude. Sarah Weese, however, slid the knife clean through in a single motion. The cheese was felled like a tree. And although Sarah Weese and I drifted apart, my snow days in high school spent with other friends in coffee shops or at the movies or sulking around the aisles of Kroger's buying stale candy, I always remembered this prowess of hers. She could open a bag of microwave popcorn and give flight to a perfect plume of steam. I'd scald myself, drop the bag, scatter its contents, curse.

Later, when I moved to Oaxaca, I watched women on the street carve mangoes into flowers. They'd peel the fruit in one slick rotation, the peel removed almost as if it'd never been there, as if it'd gotten away with a crime. Then they'd rotate the stick that sustained the mango, their hands barely moving, slitting crosswise into the gleaming yellow muscle until suddenly it became a flower. They did this over and over, dousing the mango flowers in chamoy and handing them to passersby like me, who so quickly devolved into a sticky pulpy mess that my husband was embarrassed to be walking with me.

Being in Mexico constantly reminds me of how useless my body is as a refined tool. I am a great runner; I can outpace and outlast many men. My body can tear up a 5K and strain itself to near vomiting to win a DVD player. And as a crude instrument for schlepping cheese sandwiches to the tops of mountains, my body thankfully works very well. But there is a brute, banal straightforwardness to running or hiking: lurch your body forward, keep it moving, faster, harder. The trembling elation after a backpacking trek or a run is testament to the fundamental clumsiness of these motions, the way they jolt and jar the body, straining muscles and releasing sweat and pushing all systems to the max.

In Oaxaca, people wield their bodies as instruments in the performance of distinct, elegant functions. The señoras, above all: they pound tortillas between their palms with a flat kissing sound and then, just as quickly and with just as much force, press them between metal plates and slide them onto the comal. No motion has more weight than any other, none appears to require strain or self-awareness. I am not romanticizing this, getting all heady with the copal smoke and rhapsodizing about the time when women used to spend twelve hours a day preparing meals. I once met a woman in a Oaxacan pueblo who got up at 4:00 a.m. to begin making a breakfast her husband would eat at 8:00, and while she seemed cheerful enough, I am wary of projecting a nostalgic wonder onto her.

Rather, I'm compelled by the physical knowledge apparent and contained within these daily tasks, a learning in the muscles that also indicates a certain type of relationship with the world, a sensual understanding of it: the mass of which it's composed, the materials, their reliability and unique volatility. Historically, we associate cartography with men: explorers projecting themselves onto the landscape, hacking their way up rivers, graphing their exploits on crumpled paper. The topography of women is more intimate and largely uncharted, unheralded: it is an everyday geography of masa and children's ropy bodies, nopales sheared of their needles, the rough newness of a towel from which the last drop of moisture has been wrung.

This is a way of reading the world, of both mapping and navigating it. It is a sure and unspoken learning of one's surroundings that is perhaps more seamless and intimate than that of great men. Its glories are often ignored as boring or shameful or dull, too quotidian and taken for granted to be noticed, and taking place not out in the open, on summits and plains, but in the milk caves of huddled intimacies.

Perhaps because I have always striven not for the accomplishment of perfectly baked bread but the soaring exceptionalism of a conquered peak, I suck at most tasks that demand dexterity. Maybe some innate resistance to perceived femininity slips the egg through my fingers, compels me to chomp at the mango like a medieval king working on a lamb leg. I have done nothing to try to improve this utter lack of manual ability. I have gotten along just fine without it for many years, walking down the street with beans on my face, making soups of lopsided vegetables. And for the most part I am no better at any of the quotidian tasks of physical labor—the buttering of bread, the mopping of floors—than I was ten years ago.

One summer night a few months into motherhood, however, I realize that a new physical prowess has emerged stealthy and jaguarlike from my clumsiness and overtaken me, in spite of myself. I do not know it is there until, in the diffuse glow of moonlight, with a poised, tensile delicacy and care, I lay my sleeping baby on the bed.

For an instant I hover above her, utterly still, my body a heat and a presence saying, *It's okay, it's okay, it's okay.* I have one hand on her back, the fingers lightly splayed, a touch like a leaf resting on grass. When she lifts her head a bit in protest I, without thinking, increase my touch by an infinitesimal fraction, directing into it every ion of my energy: *Please let me drink this beer and check Twitter sleep baby sleep.* It works. She settles, her body relaxes. I inch away as if in mendication, glide soundlessly off the bed, tiptoe to the door, and ease it shut in a slow, practiced, fluid motion.

My God, I think. *Where did this grace come from?*

I see then that my body has learned the geography of the baby the way that the aproned women on the corners know mangoes and the *abuelas* know tortillas and Sarah Weese knew cheese.

The material weight of the baby, her movements, the subtleties of her acquiescence or resistance, are a knowledge I've cultivated without ever realizing it. Or rather, I've realized it without respecting it as knowledge. I don't begin to do so until I notice the way other mothers, whose kids are grown, retain the corporeal memory of the myriad physical details of taking care of children. They possess this in a rote way, without nostalgic or purposeful aim, but from time to time they recognize it with a sense of wonder and self-respect. My stepmom, for example, changing a diaper. Describing it, she flings her hands around in a series of crisscrossed, mind-boggling Xs. "Wham wham wham!" she says. "Done!" It is a spot-on reenactment of a wriggling newborn's diaper change. It comes right back, she explains with the satisfaction of recalling mastery.

Mothers rely intensely on their bodies to interpret and respond to the signals of their yet-speechless infants. In doing so, they are forced to get in touch with a physical realm that is animal in its intuition. In the way great trainers can affect a horse's canter with the slightest shift of their hips, mothers curve their palms to cup fragile heads, taper their rocking to imperceptible levels to coax peace. They must read signs most people do not recognize as signs, or even movements. They learn this language because it allows them to have a fucking break from it all to watch *Parenthood* and eat Cheez-Its with their significant others, please. But also because their bodies take over their nagging minds, their impulses, the selves they thought were so solid and unbendable.

In the very beginning I am incredibly awkward at breastfeeding. My baby is great, a natural, and for this I am so thankful. But I need about fifteen precisely arranged pillows and a support system for my elbow and my husband standing by with a glass of water to tilt to my mouth, since I cannot possibly devote a finger to anything other than the exact affixation of baby to boob. Little by little I gain proficiency, I recognize the tingly avalanche of letdown, I stop fearing I am going to suffocate my baby with my own tremendously inflated bosom.

Two months in, I can breastfeed while vacuuming and reading a novel. I twist my baby around with the fearless know-how of a master swordsman, and voilà, there she is, latched, while I chat on Skype and fold socks. I can tell from the slightest turn of her lip if she wants to nurse, or to switch sides, or if she is desperate for sleep and can't get it without the help of my chest. She is a physical language I have learned to speak.

Then after I've put the baby to sleep and marveled at her head nuzzled just so in the crux of my arm, the mastery of my calming her into the cool ease of rest, I emerge from our bedroom and promptly drop a bag full of eggs. "Fucking shithead piece of crapola!" I shout. I've somehow managed to smear one down the wall, despite dropping the bag pretty much directly to the ground. The house has a vague eggy smell for days.

I seem to have gained a new corporeal sense only in areas pertaining to the soft, sweet, sticky body of my baby. And as has been the case with many other unanticipated changes of motherhood, I've developed a new respect for women's knowledge, for all of the seemingly tiny, insignificant tasks women have performed throughout thousands of years in relationship with the world around them, in the sustenance of life. We can appreciate these tasks when they are codified as work or expertise and performed by men: chefs, say, or surgeons or architects. But there is also an architecture and a surgery and an artistry to everyday life, and while I respect that there is not the same training or the same weight in the latter, it is another type of learning, unrecognized, largely unvalued, carried in the bodies of women.

But my point is not a political one. The skills developed in the body by taking care of a baby are a gift, a way of being in the world, and a way of connecting with all the women—and some men—who have learned these skills before. They are a chance, as is all of motherhood in certain instances, to dig down below all the self-conscious assertion of everyday life to a more intimate, instinctual, animal level, of poop and vomit, sure, of milk and little necks creased with prune puree, but also of a physical elegance like that of an alligator slipping into a stream.

Sometimes I anticipate a future when this knowledge will be recognized, reactivated: ten years from now when I'll hold a friend's baby, or my brother's baby, and think with pride and maybe nostalgia and maybe relief of these years and their total immersion. It is not unlike the anticipation I used to feel while living and working in foreign countries, dreaming of the day when I'd look back and remember the blue-lit morning beach, the sharp scent of anise in the air. It is infanthood as a country, mapped by a mother's body.

On a drive from Columbus to the farm one afternoon, my mom calls to check up on me and mentions cooking chicken tetrazzini just before my birth. For the remainder of the drive I think of chicken tetrazzini baking in the oven, myself in my mom's belly, her anticipation of my arrival. Only with my own baby can I understand that physical connection, that craving, the elemental biological nature of it. To be pregnant and to mother are to live at the level of those basic elements that in anti-quated biology textbooks were called "humours": blood, bile, chicken casseroles topped with Ritz crackers. These become more essential than ideas, stories, conversations: the swelling scent, the growing baby, the teeming body. To live at that level is to find boredom superfluous: the beating heart, the churning arteries cannot be boring or not boring. It is to live in total absorption with another, the thoughtlessness and timelessness of whole afternoons lost in a tangle of sheets.

I often have the sensation of living a moment simulta-neously from two bodily perspectives: my own and the baby's. When I hold her to me and look down at her I have the uncanny feeling of also looking up at myself; I sense her tiny wriggling body as my own, and so too her heat-seeking mouth, smelling my chest, and I am a single-minded being groping for warmth and milk, lulled by the tremendous comfort of a mother's proximity, while I also feel from a distance my own body relax with the knowledge of what she needs, with the power to take care of her and to feel as she feels. When she finally lets go and sleeps, the deep sleep where her whole body goes slack and her little limbs tumble around like a doll's, I too slip for a moment into the delicious relief of temporary oblivion. Her sensations eclipse mine like the sun slid-ing over the moon, leaving only the tiniest sliver, tinier, tinier, until for an instant the two merge in a total black-ness that eliminates the rest of the world.

The only other time I've had such a clairvoyant sense of another person's experience is in sex, whose overpowering physical intimacies share more with maternal connection than we tend to acknowledge. The tie between mother and baby is not lusty or erotic, but it is carnal: in the pressing of skin to skin, the synchronizing of heartbeats, the shared sweat, is the same blurriness of bodies, the same desire to inhabit another body and lose oneself in it, as in the obliterating moment of orgasm. The baby slides around atop me in the bathtub, her skin slippery with soap and so new it seems to have just come out of some silken pod; the baby and I are snuggled up tight in the dark as she nurses to sleep, her legs twined around mine; the baby dozes in her back carrier, her drool-covered cheek pressed heavily to my neck, ululations coming in little puffs from her mouth as she soothes herself into further sleep.

"Everything," Rilke extolled, "is gestation and then bringing forth."

Breastfeeding on the front porch one clear afternoon, I taste a blackberry—that is, I don't just eat a blackberry expecting blackberry taste. Looking out at the proscenium of summer sky over the humming stage of woods and pasture, I tend to think that maybe I've just never paid this type of attention. The blackberry has been another layer in a multilayered reality. But when I spend the majority of my day sitting with a baby at my breast, my world limited to a series of delicate one-handed reaches and careful crab walks, my brain soft and dreamy with oxytocin, I notice only one flavor at a time, or I don't consciously notice at all. I settle into my boredom as the day settles into its changing airs and clouds, until the baby pulls abruptly off the breast as she tends to do, sending a little jolt of pain through my nipple and leaning her head back in pure satisfaction, a dribble of milk running down her chin.

THE LAKE

THE YEAR I TURNED TWENTY, my dad drove the nine hours from Columbus, Ohio, to Madison, Wisconsin, to pick me up from college for the summer. He came in a van freckled with duct tape and coaxed into continued operation by pure Dad scrappiness. On the way back, we talked about the young adult novel he was writing, about a boy on the cusp of adolescence whose father has just died in a tractor accident on a North Dakota farm. Outside, the Midwest streamed by in golds and periwinkle blues. Just before Chicago, the van thumped, groaned, and began to expire. It ground to a terrible slowness, amplified by the cars whizzing around us. Somehow, Dad steered it onto a tiny triangle of asphalt between I-90 and the off-ramp to I-94, where it finally fell silent and died. "Well," Dad said, "I'll tell you what. That couldn't have worked out any better."

This is my dad's timeless refrain, his summary of any not-entirely-catastrophic catastrophe. Robberies, rejections, breakdowns, breakups: each ultimately comes round to an I'll-tell-you-what. He has perfected his timing, making his pronouncement at precisely the moment when calamity becomes comically absurd and transforms into family folklore. You've been thrown over the handlebars of a used mountain bike with hypersensitive brakes that Dad scored for fifty dollars? "Whoo boy," Dad announces, "good thing we were out here on these campground roads and not in the city. Tell you what: couldn't have worked out any better."

The I'll-tell-you-what is part of an enduring Dad faith, a philosophy embedded in his being like crystal in granite. To him, each potentially dire incident is a precedent for a new awareness. He is so skilled at giving a sense of meaningful inevitability to unexpected plot twists that, growing up, I never recognized his story as an I'll-tell-you-what story. I didn't feel the weight of his loss, his own dire moment; his life was not marked by regrets or wanting of redemption. He constructed for me such a sturdy sense of independence that I never saw his sacrifices as such, never thought of them as laying the groundwork for my own life until I became a writer, and a mother.

It was a mark of my dad's yet-to-be-rewarded faith in me that, when I was thirty-one, recently bestowed a highly impractical graduate degree in creative writing, and subsequently jobless, he invited me and my husband to move into a cabin on his forty-acre farm. If my life has been an exercise in stretching my dad's trust—cohabiting my final year of college with a former professor ten years my senior; backpacking alone across South America; getting engaged to a man he'd never met; relocating on a whim to China—this is perhaps the time I have most tested its elasticity. Red Hawk Farm has become Dad and my stepmom Meg's lifeblood, embodying the vision and purpose and sense of mission they lacked in their professional lives, and the personal fulfillment they often postponed or set aside as parents.

This farm is where my dad wants to die, amid the Ohio woods, the swaying grasses of the pastures, the darting blue jays and chickadees, the goofy ululations of wild turkeys, the meandering creek bedded with deep-blue slate. Here, he has begun to write again, taking up poetry at age sixty-two. Here is where he circles back to the dream he had as a young man, and here is where I am beginning to recognize the enormity of what he has granted me: the freedom, independence, and courage to pursue a creative calling he sacrificed for family. Here is where I will start my own family and where I will confront the meaning of that calling: if and how and why I am committed to it, what it means when I have a baby to raise, what to make of its filial significance and heft.

• • •

My dad grew up without a father. He was two when Earl Menkedick died of meningitis, and my grandmother stared down the nuns who wanted to collect him and his brother, Bill. Grandma took a full-time job as a receptionist at an insurance company. The German midwestern stoicism that steeled her against what could have been the all-consuming pain of grief also prevented her from expressing overt affection for her boys; she never told them "I love you." She placed her faith in hard work and education. My dad went on to become the valedictorian of his high school and won a full scholarship to Northwestern. He showed up wide eyed and idealistic in 1960s Chicago, the token working-class midwestern proof of meritocracy. He wanted to study English, to work in social justice.

Yet he quickly found himself alienated and lonely, unsure of how to be around so many kids who came from much-wealthier backgrounds and took in stride their roles as students at an elite university. He was out of place, vulnerable; he read T. S. Eliot by the wind-whipped lake. A year into college, he dropped out, returned to Cincinnati, married my mother, and had my sister. He gave up the sweeping ideals of literature and the sixties to become a father. Over the next decade he worked nights at a Cincinnati grocery store, putting first my mom and then himself through college, earning a master's in English and a master's in math from the University of Cincinnati.

I was born in 1982; one year later, my parents divorced. My dad moved out, and I went with him while my eleven-year-old sister stayed with my mom. This was, and is, highly unconventional, and now that I am a parent, I cannot imagine what my dad must have been thinking. He packed up his life and took a baby with him to a tiny basement apartment on the edge of Cincinnati's crack-addled ghetto. He planted morning glories, built a wooden playground in a backyard the size of a horse's stall, fed me and dressed me and performed the thousand daily rituals of parenting, alone and heartbroken.

My memories from that time are colored in the washed-out blues and striated yellows of old film photos: the playground at Fairview Park in winter, me in a woolly face mask that makes me look like a miniature serial killer, summiting a slide in tiny hiking boots; or me sprawled on the knobby rug—abhorrent in the way only seventies rugs can be—hugging the dog; or toddling up the street in an ill-fitting snowsuit and scraggly hair, this photo stuck to a piece of scrap paper with Dad's cheeky caption beneath: *Will you help this child?* I remember the extraordinary gift of a green Care Bear, and the precise moment I looked up and met Dad's eyes as he handed it to me; remember an illustration on the wall, a red smear with black eyes, which he called the Boogeyman; remember reading *The Giving Tree* and choosing our own giving tree in the park, a flowering cherry overlooking the Ohio River. But these memories must have all been from later, when I was four or five, and are layered atop the ones suggested by the photos to create the impression of that time.

Now I see those years through a parent's eyes. *Holy crap*, I think, *I was a toddler.* I would have been digging through drawers, wobbling around on my hammy thighs searching for electrical cords and balls of dog hair, smearing beans on the walls and wailing with protest when my face was washed. I would have been waking up fussy at 2:00 a.m. and whacking my dad on the head at 5:00 sharp to start the day. "I rocked you to sleep listening to Raffi," Dad told me years ago, and I found that sweet and quaint. I felt a tender affection for "Baby Beluga" and "Down by the Bay" and cheery bearded Raffi in his giant banana suit on the cover of *Bananaphone*. But now I know what this means. It means that drippy, sluggish exhaustion like a thousand marionette strings tugging you down, and suppressing frustration at being woken for the tenth time in two hours and feeling stabs of despair as you lift the baby from her crib, and the surprising, sweet heaviness of her head nestled into your shoulder, and singing and singing until you no longer exist, nothing exists but blackness and warmth, and finally you soften your song into sleep. The more my baby grows, and I play that role for her—waking with her; racing after her as she takes off with a measuring cup for the open door; walking, rocking, soothing for hours through teething and fevers and fears—the more stunned I am by the magnitude of what my dad did for me.

Taking care of an infant leaves lasting physical impressions: the way my sister instinctively starts to rock when handed the baby, even once the baby is a year old, and the way a friend of mine's boyfriend, who had two children by age twenty-four, jutted out his hip and said, "You'll be like this, all the time, in a year or so." He was right, and I think of this each time I thrust out that hip and set my baby astride it, feeling part hen, part mom. This is muscle memory, a rewiring of the body and mind. On a drive down Highway 1 in California with Jorge and the baby, I realize that infanthood is a place, a very small place, no bigger than ten square feet and sometimes only the size of a couch or a bathtub or two warm bodies clutched together, which parents occupy completely for several intense years in spite of how far-reaching they believe their gaze or range to be. Outside, the sea is undulating a sparkling crystalline blue and smashing white spray against the cliffs, the beaches are slivers of toasted almond, the bridges offer glimpses of Pacific between the flip books of stone rails, but try as I may to be swept away with awe I am too busy reading *Dónde Está el Ombliguito?* and proffering silicone broccoli. I am fanning Cheerios like pearls on my palm. I am making expressions of shock and fascination as I demonstrate two blocks coming together and pulling apart, I am bonking a water bottle on my head and saying, *"Ag-ua, ag-ua."* The baby has been in the car for five hours already and is willing to play along with this road-trip plan provided the entertainment is steady and enthusiastic. Even in the downtimes when she is gnawing an apple slice and I can trace the brilliant static of waves all the way to the horizon, I am not lost in the landscape as I once would have been. I am instead in the country of motherhood, and it is no bigger than arm's reach.

I have a new respect for anyone who has taken on the responsibility of infanthood, who has put in that time day in and day out, handing the plastic spoon back and forth for hours, guiding the unsteady feet up and down the step over and over, before eating an entire box of Cheez-Its and passing out. My dad did this for me, and he did it without ever revealing his own pain and loss. I did not realize until decades later that during this time Dad was also building himself back up. He had been broken, a vision of himself and an understanding of his life had crumbled, and with me in those Cincinnati years he was going through a wrenching change. Later, my sister would tell me about finding him sobbing in the kitchen of the Pleasant Ridge house in the year before the divorce. She would tell me, too, about seeing him hard at work before the typewriter.

I knew that Dad had written a novel in his midtwenties, about the night shift at a Cincinnati grocery store and working-class midwestern culture; that he'd received encouraging letters from publishers in New York; that after the divorce he'd thrown out the only copy. But I had never pictured him in the day-to-day absorption of the writer, living the writing life, and I had never pictured him racked by sobs: the only time I'd seen him cry was the day he dropped me off at college in Madison. He insulated me from his dreams, disappointments, and reconciliations; he never implicated me or suggested that his life could have been otherwise.

But taking charge of me, I finally come to understand when I have my own daughter, might have marked the end of the possibility of his being a full-time writer. He moved into that frenetic, insomniac country of infanthood with his whole heart and soul. He took me backpacking all over Ohio, through the Red River Gorge and the Blue Ridge Mountains in Kentucky, into the Great Smoky Mountains in Tennessee. I was two, three, four years old, with a pudgy belly and a stuffed unicorn creatively dubbed "Uni." He hiked through his grief, shedding it in the dappled shade of midwestern forests, showing me the surprise dart of a salamander from under a lifted stone. He instilled in me a love for the woods. The woods, that distinctly Ohioan place: not forest, not regal pines or shimmering birches, but sturdy ash and smooth-barked maple, black walnut, and American elm. For my tenth birthday, I asked for a backpacking trip, and Dad obliged. We hiked to a lake and took pictures of ourselves leaping from an overhanging rock into the water; we fished for bluegill at dusk.

Dad married my stepmom, Meg, when I was five, and the following year Jackson was born. Dad settled into a career as a scientist at a research institute and bought a house in Columbus. The dream of writing, nurtured first at Northwestern and then later in working-class fatherhood in Cincinnati, was once again set aside for the practicalities of supporting a family in a nice neighborhood, putting three children through college, taking everyone on vacations to Michigan, and stopping for breakfast at Frisch's, where, growing up, he'd eaten out once a year with his mother.

I, meanwhile, began to develop my own interest in writing, first with my brilliantly titled second-grade literary debut, *Animals,* which featured, as one might intimate, a host of creatures in their native environments. In the best example to date of my budding egoism, I dedicated *Animals* to myself. (On the second page was printed "This book is dedicated to _____," and in the blank I penciled *Me.*) I swept the summer reading challenge at our local library, racing through nearly the entire Baby-Sitters Club oeuvre in two months. In high school, I won the local Rotary 4-Way Speech Test Contest with a missive that railed against homophobia and compared it to the Holocaust, opening with the subtle, allusive line "Six million Jews." I made it to the state finals the following year with a speech about Ray Bradbury's *Fahrenheit 451,* this one more finely tuned, with invectives against consumerism blended with wispy, softly voiced odes to the moon.

Dad came with me to that second Rotary competition,

just as he had come to the first, sitting through twenty-some speeches moralizing against the evils of marijuana and teen pregnancy. We drove to Finley, Ohio, where finals were held in a small, fluorescent-lit room in a redbrick building. I went first. About a minute into my speech, I blanked out. Just blanked out completely, falling into total silence like tumbling over a cliff. It lasted maybe thirty seconds; it seemed eternal. Then I picked up where I'd left off. I delivered the rest of the speech exactly as rehearsed, thanked the Rotary Club, and sat down wearing a rictus of forced composure. My dad's compassion was written all over his face. In the parking lot I broke down, taking sobbing sips from my complimentary water bottle. All that work and I had screwed it up. I came in fifth out of five. A future business major—a business major! I wept—had taken the gold.

"I'm so proud of you," he said. "You finished with dignity." I think he was prouder of me for having failed and persevered with grace than he would have been had I won. On the ride home, he tried to cheer me up. "I'll letcha get whatever you want from Walmart!" he offered.

"Wow, Dad," I said.

"Okay, for under twenty dollars," he added.

After I'd selected my random consolation prize, surely a Boyz II Men CD or hideous sweatshirt, and we were approaching the highway on one of those nowhere Ohio exits, all cornfields and country roads, he said, "You and I have something special. We grew up together." It was the only time he has referenced our bond, and it came on the heels of my first disappointment as a writer.

I took it for granted that my dad was using the royal *we* of parents. "We don't smash eggs on the dog, do we?" "We *love* spinach, don't we?": that instinctive, knee-jerk *we* that blurs the parent's identity with the child's to teach social mores or maintain a veneer of politeness over seething frustration or express family solidarity. But I see now that this *we* was genuine, implying him as much as me. I grew up, and he grew up, too; he molted as I am molting now, letting go of past givens, rewriting himself, immersed in the natural world.

My dad was raised without a father, and became an exemplary one. He gave his life to filling the gap in his own childhood, where a man never sat in the audience and applauded for him in spite of his humiliating fail-ure, never listened to him for hours on afternoon drives through endless midwestern cornfields. I want to give mine now to filling the space where his novel may have been published, where he may have achieved the glory of recognition for a poem. Maybe we all long for some part of our past that was never fulfilled; we carry a lack in our bones. We seek it in smell or touch or landscape, stories or mementos or photographs, or subconsciously in amor-phous cravings. For my dad this was the experience of having a father, of being fathered, and for me this is the novel of his twenties, all the novels that went unwritten as he played Frisbee on the lawn and fixed my bike and drove me night after night to play practice.

But whereas my dad's devotion to fatherhood was almost entirely selfless, born of sacrifice, my dedication to writing is born of the independence, strength, and drive he nurtured in me. The only sacrifice I have made for the freedom to write is that of furniture and a decent haircut. Instead I have asked others to make sacrifices for me: asked my husband to move to the United States so that I could attend graduate school, asked my parents to let me camp out on their beloved land. Now that I have a baby, the stakes of these sacrifices are rising: Can I claim that my writing is so important, so central, that it might mean I lack money for decent health care? Can I ask my husband to watch the baby for several hours each day in lieu of taking paying work, or much-needed time off, so that I can write highfalutin essays about the culture of Spanglish? Is staking out my impractical artistic mission amid financial insecurity and the all-consuming years of early parenthood empowering, a defiance of the centuries-old pressure on women not to demand too much, or simply selfish hedonism?

The house looks as though someone has flipped it upside down and shaken it, we're surviving off cans of refried beans, the poor dog is curled beneath the walnut tree in a state of shocked despair, and I am looking up shades of orange (Mahogany! Vermilion! Atomic tangerine!). I might as well be stopping for a cupcake in a hurricane.

And so for the first time I understand the lure of giving up, of declaring it officially impossible and not worth it and taking a job as a park ranger. I have failed enough now to understand how unrealistic it is to expect the kind of success that would actually support a family, the kind of success that would provide tangible and objective proof of the worthwhileness of continuing. I am worn down and exasperated with all the rejection and the uncertainty and the starting-from-scratch ambiguity of each day, and family is the best and simplest excuse to say, *Enough*.

On one of the drives back up to Madison, eighteen-hour round-trip journeys my dad undertook to drop me off, we stopped in Evanston. "I'll show you my old haunting grounds," Dad offered. It was summer, and the lake was a glinting cobalt blue, foamy at the edges, framed by tawny statuesque buildings. "I used to take walks here," he told me. "I read poetry." The narrow beaches were still emptied of students, the piers lonely and meager before the vast lake.

Growing up, I had taken it as a point of pride that Dad spurned Northwestern, that he was accepted into and then rejected that rich kids' school and still made so much of his life, that he never nursed bitterness or a greater-than-thou attitude and went on to become the most intelligent, gentle, and respected person I knew. I had endowed his story with a Menkedick pedigree: not needing—and in fact triumphing in spite of—the Man. I had taken what he had given up so much for granted that

I'd forgotten he'd given it up, and like anything given up, it lived on as the not-done, the not-realized, even if only in the very back of his mind on Sundays, or during tedious drives to Cincinnati, or walking the dog on certain spring evenings.

At twenty, during our impromptu detour, I finally felt what it meant to give something up. This trip was my first adult intimation of loss, of the fact that certain decisions are irrevocable even if they come round to the I'll-tell-you-what. I saw the ivy on the patrician stone houses and the stoic grandeur of the lake and understood that here my dad had felt longing, had once held the promise of becoming an English professor or a poet or an organizer of city youth or all of these, but had ultimately not become any. In this moment my dad became for me human, fallible, and my relationship with him lost some of its childlike one-sidedness and gained a more adult inflection of empathy and nuance.

Then we drove on, and surely I soliloquized with great pomposity about an obscure development in environmental history, and he had a double gin and tonic at Genna's on the Square, and we walked around Madison's tamer, gentler lake before we called it a night, well-sweetie-time-to-hit-the-hay.

It is too easy to extrapolate from my dad's experience of loss the permission to live my life unfettered in the noble pursuit of literature, quality dinnerware and savings be damned. Still, in the way Dad trusts me even in the most uncertain circumstances, the way he urges me on and persuades me to have faith even with rejection after rejection, I sometimes sense that moment by the lake. In some ways, the more impractical writing begins to seem—another failed book, a baby, a plan to move to California—the more I sense that my dad wants me to keep at it. I don't feel this as pressure or an obligation, and I know he wouldn't judge me if I were to say, "You know what, I'm taking this nine-to-five job at a nice middlebrow magazine and we're buying a house." He'd likely be ecstatic for me to host Thanksgiving and stop calling him about the dead mouse in the kitchen. His quiet influence is more about extending permission, believing in the indefinable and experiential and existential stakes of art, and hoping that belief—and the part of oneself that believes—can be validated. My dad understands what it means to struggle for a creative, unconventional life, and he respects that struggle. No one ever modeled it for him or listened to him in his moments of doubt and urged him on; he had to tackle the massive and intimidating prospect of failure far earlier than I did, and without family who understood either the risk or the decision not to take it. He understands both.

On a walk through the winter woods in the middle of my pregnancy, when I am kvetching about the impending rejection of my latest work, feeling despondent with yet another failure and the purposelessness of this whole endeavor, my dad says, gently, "You know, big deal. That's what the Buddhists say. I mean, maybe you publish one great poem your whole life. And big deal!" He's wearing his old down coat and his scruffy hat and his muck boots, shrugging in a foot of snow. He's not being derisive or flippant or dismissive. He's letting me off the hook, reminding me what matters. We are out for a walk in the fresh afternoon cold, and soon I will have a baby, for whom he will build a padded wooden rocking chair like the one he rocked me to sleep in so many nights. In the end this whole endeavor is worth so much more and less than that.

As I move into early motherhood, I find myself less and less able to nurture the gallant fantasy of fulfilling his dream of being a writer. It becomes less and less clear what that fulfilled dream—my own or his—looks like and consists of. His dream was likely part the letter of acceptance from the major publisher and part the successful depiction of the guy on third shift named Frank who named his two sons Frank and Frank, the satisfaction of paying close attention to the relationships and sensations and emotions that compose everyday life. He went on to do this in other ways: memorizing birdsongs, turkey hunting by himself at 5:00 a.m., watching his children discover the world.

My own dream, meanwhile, is less and less the proverbial carrot and more the immediate desire to note that this morning I fed the baby a wild black raspberry, felt her muggy, gummy little mouth on my fingers, and turned to see her round face, smiling its guileless baby grin, tilted askew to meet mine. At dinner the other night I told Jorge that for the first time I understand writing as a struggle toward clarity; in the past, I've mostly known what I wanted to say, had an idea how to say it. Now I don't. I gather up the everyday and stir it around on the page, working it and working it until the water runs clear.

"It is a kind of mystery that for people who have no experience of enlightenment, enlightenment is something wonderful," Suzuki writes. "But if they attain it, it is nothing. But yet it is not nothing. Do you understand? For a mother with children, having children is nothing special."

At a time when I am still figuring out how to keep a small, vulnerable human alive, I am less and less able to define why writing matters, and yet I begin to write like I mother: out of bedrock necessity. The baby's diaper needs to be changed and I change it. I need to write and I write. I don't write because I think I will lose a part of myself if I stop, because I think becoming a park ranger will cause my soul to wither with the spurning of art. In fact I think I might live a healthy, happy everyday life: bake more pies, write more letters, stop driving Jorge mad by leaving balled diapers on the rug. I write not because I have some new gleaming sense of purpose, or even because the literature of motherhood hoisted me out of my own moments of despair and made me want to give that gift to another stranded soul. I sure as hell don't write to make money. I know less and less of why I write, and the less I know the more compelled I am to do it, the more I drive at it the way the hummingbird drives with a jet roar into the hostas, making me duck each time.

In *Zen in the Art of Archery*, Eugen Herrigel, a professor of philosophy living in Japan, recounts his quest to learn archery and, through it, Zen. Herrigel is constantly trying to find some trick, a formula, for pulling off the perfect shot, but his teacher insists that he not shoot, that instead, when the bow is at its point of highest tension, he wait until the arrow shoots itself. Of course, this is maddening for the poor pupil, the kind of maxim that makes a frustrated writer want to say, *Screw it, I'm starting a mommy blog.* Herrigel tries again and again, unable to wait, succumbing to quivering muscles, always attempting to discern the right moment instead of letting go. And then one day he does it, unawares. He looses the arrow unconsciously, having disappeared into the postures and rhythms he's learned so well. He writes, "It is necessary for the archer to become, in spite of himself, an unmoved center. Then comes the supreme and ultimate miracle: art becomes 'artless,' shooting becomes not-shooting, a shooting without bow and arrow; the teacher becomes a pupil again, the Master a beginner, the end a beginning, and the beginning perfection."

I am unsure whether the hours I manage to carve

out at my desk with leftover peanut butter pie, mentally shredded from intermittent waking, could be qualified as perfection, but from time to time slogging away I feel myself become this center. It is a return to the emptiness I experienced for the first time when I was pregnant: a feeling of calm, clarified seeing without any grasping. The part of my brain that is perpetually waiting for the baby's slightest whimper, the part that is aware I'm in a barn in a hot green Ohio summer struggling to write to the tune of the whirring fan: all fade and I am nothing but the play of words. I am not going anywhere or aiming at anything; I am not myself so much as I am a hollowness. I am rung by the world like a bell; I am breathed, as Herrigel puts it, instead of breathing.

Mostly, however, I write like a mule schleps its load up a mountain. There is no misty aura of glory or romance, and oftentimes it's a slow and tedious hoofing for my hormone-boggled brain, and I stop every ten minutes for Cheez-Its. I defend my writing time, though, with teeth. Jorge and I get in the worst, longest-smoldering fights of our relationship about this time, whose practicality I cannot justify. He is the one earning the money. He is the one whose time is billable, who actually pays the bills with his wedding photography, although often he'd rather be shooting documentaries about rodeo riders in the Mexican Sierra. And he washes dishes, fries bacon, does laundry, walks with the baby around the yard saying, *Yes, the birdie house, yes, the leaf, oh, yes, what a nice rock*. It requires a terrible and terrific arrogance for me to claim three hours to hash out a half-coherent treatise on the gestation periods of walruses: an arrogance not only in the immediate domain of my family but in a larger, universal sense, to imagine that fitting life into language matters when I have now lived the reality of birth and the pressing need of a hot little mouth.

The preciousness of that time, the fact that it is so contested and fraught with the weight of what is not being done with it, have forced my hand: I have to admit that I believe in art. Not as a lofty ideal, a form of salvation or elevation or sublime otherness, but as a way of accessing the large, old emotions and mysteries within the everyday, a way of being first shown to me by my dad. A consciousness. One that, for me, is equal to motherhood in its eradication of the self and the worldly, and yet is simultaneously of the world, composed of paper coffee cups in cheap hotels and the ragged snores of dogs, of quesadillas and the soundless descent of the perfectly pitched beanbag into the cornhole. And so I hunker down and defend my territory, lash out from it like a threatened bear. And yet the time itself is not some great march toward progress or glory; whereas in the past I was always working for a goal, an MFA, publication, awards, recognition, now I simply work.

Still, the pragmatic is constantly encroaching from all sides, with its spears of financial, familial anxiety: How in the world will we ever afford college? Preschool? A car that isn't perpetually on the verge of collapse? Ignoring these questions would be delusional and unfair, although I can fight against the overwhelming American pressure to conform, to assume that the only way to raise a child is in a nice suburban home, bedtime at seven, soccer on Sundays, and a steadily accumulating college fund. There's nothing wrong with this; it can be a dreamy way to grow up. But there are other ways to build a life and a family that bring their own benefits: the days I spend traveling with the baby, showing her seashells, rolling around cheap hotel beds blowing raspberries into her legs, and the meaning my husband and I find in our lives, our work, our everyday, which I hope we give to her as a deep passion and priority.

Still, I'd love to be paid for my writing, to live from it. I'd love a nursery, beautiful rocking horses, actual counter space. But even as those endless, important, and tedious questions about the accumulation of wealth and status weigh heavier and harder on the everyday, I sense a more pressing need to sequester my writing from them. The stakes are higher now than ever before: either I keep it separate, I write because I have to, I read what I want to, and I figure everything else out as best I can (fellowships? ESL? second photographer to my brilliant husband?), or I give it up. Become a park ranger. Bake pies and move on. Which maybe, someday, I'll do. But for now I take my coffee and my computer to the barn, and I go until my brain hurts, until my body feels wrung out, and I keep going until up at the screen door pops Jorge's brown, bearded face: *"Te toca."* Toothy grin. In his arms is the wriggly baby, hungry for Mom, hungry for milk, and her eager pawing at my chest reminds me once again why this matters so much and not at all.

When I first move into the cabin I clear out the drawers in my dad's old wardrobe to make room for my socks. There I find dozens of frail, yellowing index cards scrawled with words like *dewlapped* and *heliotrope* and *oleaginous*. They are packed in careful, cribbed handwriting onto each card: *mucilaginous, pentapod,* and *limn; turpitude* and *fugue* and *bête noir.* All of this prodigal lyricism set aside in a dusty drawer and discovered by tired, hormonal, confused, pregnant me, so many years later. I move those cards to my own desk and begin writing again.

So does my dad. One of his first poems is about observing a man at a dressage competition in southeastern Ohio. *Why was he there?* my dad wonders in the poem, studying him. For his granddaughter or his wife, surely. Dad looks away, watches the other goings-on in preparation for the competition. When he turns back, the man is dressed in full riding regalia, ready to trot his horse into the ring. Dad sees the man: "his own person, my contemporary / And I see the tenderness and care / Was for his own precious self."

Finally, after forty years of child-rearing, he can spend

the whole morning writing. We are now writing in tandem, some five hundred feet apart, listening to the same birdsongs, looking at the same stretch of woods.

Dad was not present at my labor, which was all female save for the blessed Jorge, who navigated a scene of six women—one screaming, bleeding, and panting; three comforting and soothing and pacing; two guiding and directing—with his preternatural grace. Dad stayed at the farm and waited for updates. When I'd started to experience intense pain while still only five centimeters dilated, Meg called Dad to fill him in.

Later, he tells me that at this point he went upstairs and did tonglen meditation. The purpose of tonglen, which can be translated from the Tibetan as "giving and taking," is to take on the suffering of others, breathing it in on the in breath, and to give back happiness, breathing it out on the out breath. I think of Dad in the lotus position in his paint-splattered T-shirt and his white kneesocks, his aching foot bent beneath him, breathing in suffering and breathing out happiness in big, slow, concentrated breaths. A little over two hours later the baby is born: bright red, crying at full pitch, our healthy beautiful Elena.

There is no way to repay or to thank my dad, no act or story that can ever hope to acknowledge how he has absorbed our suffering and given his precious breath for our happiness. I can only try to emulate his gentleness with my own daughter, and to write. Write not to redeem a lost glory, as I once imagined, but to make of my life a more conscious and empathetic and open space; write not to compensate for a dearth in his life, but to become more like him.

I look at a picture my dad has on his bookshelf of him and his father. My dad is a freckled little boy in suspenders and high-waisted 1950s shorts. He stands beside his dad, a chubby-cheeked young man just back from war, who smiles as he leans on one knee toward his son. I see my dad as a child, which is to say I feel for him a motherly affection. This has begun happening since I became a mother: the cycles get muddled and move too quickly and I lose my place in them. I feel a maternal empathy and concern for my parents, a childlike adoration and need for my child. The love I feel for the little boy in my dad's old photo and the love I sense from Elena blend, indistinguishable, ever renewing.

My dad married Meg in a backyard ceremony at our house on Fairview Avenue in Cincinnati. It was an old brick house they'd bought together, with ivied front steps and a big sycamore that sprawled its palomino branches over the backyard. They exchanged vows at sunset under a white tent, and Meg's friend's band serenaded them with the Talking Heads "This Must Be the Place." Dad gamely carried a whiny me over his shoulder for the better part of the night. The following year, Jack was born in the front room of the Fairview house, and we were a family.

In those early years my dad and Meg were deep into Free Daism, an offshoot of Buddhism spawned by a Queens-born guru who went on to christen himself Adi Da and write a series of books with titles like *The Incarnation of Love* and *The Knee of Listening*. After a sex scandal and accusations of brainwashing, they realized the guru, holed up at a commune in Fiji, might be on the sketchier side of New Agey, and they left Free Daism. But the teachings, which were rooted in the fundamentals of Buddhism, stayed with them and were instilled in my brother and me as we were growing up. I remember my dad reading me a book that asked "Why is an apple an apple?" The concept seems obvious now—the random, symbolic abstraction of language—but at the time it was radical, a question that made my brain itch. There was a lot of talk of "the mystery," which was at the heart of the unanswerableness of the apple question. Having grown up Catholic and later rejected Catholicism, Meg and Dad found meaning instead in the mystery: the notion that we can't know and that we can find peace and meaning in not knowing. *Respect the mystery,* my dad used to tell me when I'd torque myself up with worry about AIDS or the flesh-eating disease or velociraptors or, later, work myself into great quandaries of adolescent self-doubt.

Language breaks down before the mystery, as I discovered trying to explain it to college boyfriends, who inevitably walked away with a notion of my parents as tie-dyed, incense-reeking, adorable Ohioans who encouraged their kids to offer orange slices to a blown-up photo of a burly New Yorker. My dad would get frustrated with me later when I grilled him about Free Daism with my writer's relentless, prodding curiosity. He was unable to neatly summarize what appealed to them, although he never regretted this time and was quick to point out that he and Meg still lived by many of the same precepts: not getting caught by desires; living a conscious, compassionate life; not fearing death.

At the farm, in early motherhood, I circle back now to the mystery. There have been many periods of my life in which I have not known where I'm headed, but never with the combination of settledness I feel now—settledness in my family and my commitments—and a new understanding of the randomness of choice. China or Portland, farm or apartment block, in the end it will all come round to the same things: coffee in the morning, books, cameras, the juggling of finances and responsibilities and competing desires within the finite container of the day. The mystery is the space between it mattering so much and it not mattering at all.

One long and tired afternoon in August, Jorge and I are beginning to have one of our fights, and at that first sharp flare that ignites all of our sensitivities, I am struck by the notion that it doesn't matter: standing on the grass, taking in the house and the cabin, I think, *Why bother*. It is not that I stumble upon that clipped, fuck-it wisdom of "life is short," that I don't want to waste time with anger. It is rather that the passionate fury of the moment seems so small and irrelevant, my life so small and irrelevant, that I can't work myself up. I don't go make oatmeal cookies for the whole family and write love letters to long-ignored friends; I just go back inside and get to work, trying to keep my back straight, watching those dreamboat storm clouds bluster in on the wind.

"Life is short" suggests that we should rush to fulfill as many of our desires as possible—make a pass at the neighbor girl, stuff ourselves with chocolate cake, drop everything to call our grandmothers—because there's not enough time and we'll be flayed by regrets. The thought of it all not mattering is different. It's more like I, myself, am a TV show I don't really care about, with the actors tearing up and ranting about dramas that seem hazy and insignificant, and so I stretch and turn the TV off and have a Kalamazoo Stout on the front porch, watching the last of the lightning bugs carve tangled streaks of incandescence through the trees.

In August, I am making a slow rotation around the cabin as I do with the baby, bringing the world into focus object by object—birdhouse, sunflower, butterfly, rock—when

I notice squash flowers blooming in our small, messy garden. My dad cruises up, as he often does with a tool or a question or just wanting to chat idly with his buddy Jorge, and I offer to make him a squash blossom quesadilla. I enter the womblike darkness of the cabin, which is simultaneously summery and holding a protective wintery musk. I set butter to sizzle in a pan. The squash flowers go in, with some cumin, salt, pepper. I press them and white cheddar between two tortillas, rub butter on both sides, heat them to a toasty brown. My dad has come in and is playing with the baby, and I say, "Try this," but his hands are full of infant, and with cheese dripping down my arm, I drop the square of quesadilla into his mouth. His eyes lift, light up.

"Wow!" he says, with his utterly genuine enthusiasm, his warmth. In my twenties I never would have envisioned this moment, in a cabin, with a baby, making a squash blossom quesadilla for my dad. In cooking for him, feeding him, I feel like the mama bird, and also for the first time like the daughter taking care of an aging parent. My dad is still capable of unloading several hundred pounds of wood and chasing a toddler around for hours (activities that inflict approximately parallel levels of exhaustion), but nonetheless in this moment I feel his mortality, which I now see is aligned with my burgeoning adulthood. I get to feed him this warm pocket of fresh flower and cheese, as he fed me redbud blossoms, crunchy sweet and fresh with dew, and hemlock tea and morel mushrooms with olive oil and garlic over spaghetti, and as later I will feed Elena crushed paneer and creamy Mexican black beans and oatmeal with blackstrap molasses. There is a different kind of knowing in this moment, which I did not have a year ago: knowing to walk slowly around the house, knowing to kneel and pluck the flower from its stem, knowing to stop and chat with my dad, knowing to offer the quesadilla and to come inside and cook it carefully, deliberately, and give it to him as a gift, knowing it is all nothing, it is all in a day. This is the mystery: moments of calm knowing that contain within them nothing larger than the everyday. And this is what I am seeking, although I don't know this, or cannot articulate it, until more than a year after Elena is born, when I am walking with her through the pastures, thumping her new running stroller over molehills and tangles of cut multiflora rose. She is being jangled to sleep, and my brain is jangling around the question of what is different about reading and writing and my understanding of them. It is summer dusk, and long sashes of peach light fall over the pastures. Phlox blooms by the walnut tree before the cabin, waving stiffly in the breeze like a stodgy Englishman trying not to seem overly excited. Without realizing it or trying, I see, I have shed the pressing need for purpose. I don't need to be able to define a book's themes, its goals, its *message*. I've developed an aversion to stories that have too clear an aim; I want the heady, dreamy immersion of novels or of stories so intimate and pressed up close to a life that they have no bigger picture. I want to feel the world called up, depicted in its contradictions and coincidences and complex schemas. I want to merge with it, with its mystery. *Why is an apple an apple?* I can only say, *I fed my dad a squash blossom quesadilla.*

The other day, Jorge got out of the shower and I was lying in bed with the baby, exhausted, listening to Andrew Bird, and Jorge, his hair plastered penguinlike to his head, towel wrapped around his brown belly, started playing the air violin. He rocked out on the strings and then moved on to the air harp, the air trumpet, the air flute, until I was laughing so hard I was coughing and the baby looked on in confusion. He left and then returned marching to the air trombone.

"Ohhhhh," says the baby, a long, almost moaning sound, when she notices something, anything: cow, gum wad stuck to the sidewalk, cigarette butt, hummingbird. "Ohhhh," her mouth a perfect O of wonderment, and she looks at me to make sure I see it, too.

One winter morning my dad comes up and knocks on the kitchen window, beside where the baby is sitting on the table in her Bumbo seat. He is wearing a fluorescent yellow knit hunting cap, and he shows the baby an egg, hoisting it up like a wild jewel extracted from the forest, grinning a big wacky grin.

During this time at the farm, I have been teaching my dad Spanish. Dad, always embarking on a new learning curve—birdsongs, dog training, mushroom hunting—

wants to learn Spanish in order to travel to Oaxaca and communicate with Jorge's family. Little by little, he and I forge our way through verb tenses, vocabulary, idioms: "for everything good, *mezcal,* and for everything bad, too." To convey unknown vocabulary I draw terrible sketches of eggplant and horses, and sometimes he switches into English without realizing it but keeps speaking in the accent of a mustachioed Mexican paramour. He is perpetually coming up with obscure words for things like small splashes in puddles of rainwater, and I am perpetually trying to bring him round to the basics of *queso* and *zapatos.*

I try to enforce a Spanish-only rule during our lessons, and sometimes this means it takes a while to get meaning across via context. Last fall, we had conversation practice while we picked apples from the two trees in the front pasture. We were squinting up at the high branches, angling baskets attached to long wooden poles, talking about family.

"*Cuántos hijos tienes?*" I asked him. How many children do you have?

"*Hijos?*" he asked.

"*Hijos,*" I said, gesturing at myself and Jack, who was listening to music in the barn nearby.

"*Hijos . . . ,*" he mused, not getting it.

"*Hijos,*" I said again, more emphatically, pointing at Jack, then myself. I tapped my chest, just over my heart. "*Soy tu hija. Somos tus hijos.*" I am your daughter. We are your children.

"Oh, *hijos!*" he said. Then slowly, deliberately, *"Tu. Eres. Mi. Hija."* He grinned with the sheepish grin he reserves for Spanish, when he must play the role of infant.

And on this clear fall day in southeastern Ohio, the spotted apples dangling like pearls from those cragged branches, my own daughter just beginning to assert herself in my belly, I wanted to say, *I'll tell you what, it couldn't have worked out any better.*

ACKNOWLEDGMENTS

When I first began writing, I labored under the cliché that art is made in beautiful, agonized solitude, the artist emerging stunned and blinking from her cave in the early evening for a stiff drink. Little by little, as I founded a magazine and became part of a community of writers, that cliché eroded. Parts of the writing process are and must be intensely solitary, but a finished work is a collaboration of influences, perspectives, insights, and criticisms. I have never felt this as acutely as I have while working on this book. The close readings and critiques of friends and editors have been essential: equally so, the efforts and sacrifices my family has made to give me the time, space, and energy to work.

Thank you to Emily Giglierano for believing in and championing this book from the start, and for her enthusiasm for my midwesternisms. An immense thank you to my editor Andrea Robinson, for her acumen, thoughtfulness, and patience, and for guiding me through this process. Thank you to my agent Jane Dystel, for her support and faith. She took me on, stuck with me, and assured me in the low moments that I would one day have a book; now I do.

I would not be half the writer I am today without the time, energy, and critical reading of *Vela's* editors, who shook me out of many complacencies, bad habits, and indulgences, and taught me to see my work anew. I want to thank in particular the brilliant Amanda Giracca and Simone Gorrindo, who have spent hundreds of hours wading through my rants and redundancies and sifting from them a few hopeful seeds, and whose readings of the first few drafts of this book helped shape it and make it possible. I am so grateful to have you as friends and colleagues; may we continue our three-hour-long Skype sessions about infant inserts and chickens and the present tense long after your babies are born. Thank you also to Jenny Williams, longtime companion on this often grim, sometimes transcendent literary path, whose camaraderie has many times saved me from nihilism.

Thank you to Mary Menkedick, the most selfless, big-hearted, awe-inspiring sister a girl could hope for, who works full-time, has two fearless soon-to-be teenagers, coaches softball, runs marathons, and still finds the time to stay up until three in the morning reading messy drafts of her little sister's motherhood book. No thank-you is big enough for you and all you give. Thank you to Jackson Menkedick for being a kindred spirit in art and life, for the shared bizarre sense of Menkedick humor, for letting me tag along on your artistic quests into the woods. I miss you. Thank you to my mom, Lois Carter, for nurturing in me a love of beauty and art; for your vivacious spurning of convention; for your loyalty, aesthetic, and sense of humor; and for your intuitive understanding of who I am. Thank you to Meg Menkedick for the care, from mittens and cheese sandwiches to Stauf's talks to those darkest moments of uncertainty: I know now how hard it is, and how sacred. Thank you to my dad for being my rock, and for your infinite patience, infinite gentleness, and wisdom.

This book would not exist if my dad and Meg hadn't sat down with my husband and me one summer night in 2013 and offered to let us live for a year in the cabin on their farm. Their gift, of both space and belief, is the most precious one I have ever received. I hope to do it justice as a writer and a mother.

Finally, thank you to Jorge Santiago, a far, far better man and husband than I deserve. I cannot imagine myself or my life without you. *Eres mi alma, mi corazón, siempre; gracias por haberme suportado tanto tiempo.* And to Elena, my sweet, sweet baby girl: my love for you is too big for this book and this life. You taught me everything worth knowing.

ALSO BY

SARAH MENKEDICK

WILD RIVER BLUES
A Vintage eBook Short

In her early thirties and an aspiring literary journalist, Sarah Menkedick joins her baby brother Jackson and his precious Honda, the "Jackwagon," for fourteen transformative days on an East Coast backpacking adventure. The two cross mountains and by the end—exhausted to the core and unshowered—they reflect on the trajectory of their lives, the music they make and listen to, the principles to which they strive, and the disillusionment one can encounter after years of doggedly pursuing a passion. With only each other for company, they escape the trappings of their material lives. Together, they learn to heal, to love, and finally—to listen to one another.

Memoir

VINTAGE BOOKS
Available wherever books are sold.
www.vintagebooks.com

MEATY

Essays

by Samantha Irby

Meaty is the widely beloved, uproarious, essay collection from edgy, smart, hilarious, and unabashedly raunchy Samantha Irby. Irby exploded onto the printed page with this debut collection of essays about trying to laugh her way through failed relationships, taco feasts, bouts with Crohn's disease, and more. Every essay is crafted with the same scathing wit and poignant candor that thousands of loyal readers have come to expect from visiting her notoriously hilarious blog, bitchesgottaeat.com.

Essays

LAB GIRL

by Hope Jahren

Geobiologist Hope Jahren has spent her life studying trees, flowers, seeds, and soil. *Lab Girl* is her revelatory treatise on plant life—but it is also a celebration of the lifelong curiosity, humility, and passion that drive every scientist. In these pages, Hope takes us back to her Minnesota childhood, where she spent hours in unfettered play in her father's college laboratory. She tells us how she found a sanctuary in science, learning to perform lab work "with both the heart and the hands." She introduces us to Bill, her brilliant, eccentric lab manager. And she extends the mantle of scientist to each one of her readers, inviting us to join her in observing and protecting our environment. Warm, luminous, compulsively readable, *Lab Girl* vividly demonstrates the mountains that we can move when love and work come together.

Memoir

THE LUNCH-BOX CHRONICLES
Notes from the Parenting Underground
by Marion Winik

With the candor and often hilarious outlook that have made her a beloved commentator on NPR, Marion Winik takes the reader on an unforgettable journey through modern parenthood, with all of its attendant anxieties and joys. A single mother with two small boys, Winik knows exactly what she's talking about, from battles over breakfast and bedtime to the virtues of pre-packaged food and weightier issues like sex education and sibling rivalry. Part memoir and part survival guide, *The Lunch-Box Chronicles* is an engaging philosophy of parenting from a staunch realist, who knows that kids and their parents both will inevitably fall far short of perfection, and that a "good enough mom" really is, in fact, good enough.

Parenting

OPERATING INSTRUCTIONS
A Journal of My Son's First Year
by Anne Lamott

It's not like she's the only woman to ever have a baby. At thirty-five. On her own. But Anne Lamott makes it all fresh in her now-classic account of how she and her son and numerous friends and neighbors and some strangers survived and thrived in that all-important first year. From finding out that her baby is a boy (and getting used to the idea) to finding out that her best friend and greatest supporter, Pam, will die of cancer (and not getting used to that idea), with a generous amount of wit and faith (but very little piousness), Lamott narrates the great and small events that make up a woman's life.

Child Care